BRACKETOLOGY

*March Madness,
College Basketball,
and the Creation of
a National Obsession*

Joe Lunardi
with David Smale

TRIUMPH
BOOKS

Library of Congress Cataloging-in-Publication Data

Names: Lunardi, Joe, author.
Title: Bracketology : March Madness, college basketball, and the creation of a national obsession / by Joe Lunardi with David Smale.
Description: Chicago : Triumph Books, 2021. | Summary: "This books is about the process and history of selecting teams into the NCAA Tournament"—Provided by publisher.
Identifiers: LCCN 2020048220 (print) | LCCN 2020048221 (ebook) | ISBN 9781629378817 (hardcover) | ISBN 9781641255806 (epub)
Subjects: LCSH: NCAA Basketball Tournament.
Classification: LCC GV885.49.N37 L86 2021 (print) | LCC GV885.49.N37 (ebook) | DDC 796.323/63—dc23
LC record available at https://lccn.loc.gov/2020048220
LC ebook record available at https://lccn.loc.gov/2020048221

This book is available in quantity at special discounts for your group or organization. For further information, contact:
　　Triumph Books LLC
　　814 North Franklin Street
　　Chicago, Illinois 60610
　　(312) 337-0747
　　www.triumphbooks.com

Printed in U.S.A.
ISBN: 978-1-62937-881-7
Design by Patricia Frey
Page Production by NordCompo

*To Don DiJulia, the MVP—Most Valuable
Person—of my alma mater and basketball career.
Everyone who knows him, knows why.*

Contents

Foreword

I've spoken with Joe Lunardi on enough occasions to know that his breadth of knowledge of every detail of every team that should be considered going into the NCAA Tournament is beyond reproach. He's relentless.

Coaches in general are relentless, whether it be in recruiting, scouting, preparation, or development. We throw all our energy and resources into trying to be successful, so I admire that trait in Joe. It's impressive and inspiring just how hard Joe works and how diligent he is. He does a new bracket for the following year immediately after the season is over. He constantly updates it in the spring and summer. Obviously, it's purely speculative, but I'm always impressed with just how accurate he is, whether that's seeding numbers or the teams that are chosen. He ends up nailing it.

Beyond correctly predicting who is going to get into that year's tournament, Joe's resources are very valuable to coaches because scheduling is such an important part of our job. Scheduling is tucked neatly behind recruiting in importance to being successful in your job as a coach. I think it would be amazing to research how many coaches look at his work and use it in regard to scheduling. He has become an extremely valuable resource.

I was an assistant at Gonzaga with Dan Monson. When he took over the head job in 1997, he changed how we scheduled at Gonzaga. We went out and aggressively tried to schedule the best opponents we could for our own experiences within the program. We felt like it would be fun for our players to play against the best teams. It also helped us grow the program.

We needed to analyze the best ways to schedule to put ourselves in the position to get strong consideration for an at-large bid. I don't think the Bracketology aspect really took hold for us until the early 2000s—long after we reached the Elite Eight in 1999 and then backed it up with two Sweet 16s in the next two years. By then I felt like we had put ourselves in that position. We were already using those types of principles, but we had no numbers to back it up. We were doing it by feel, knowing college basketball and knowing who was going to be good.

Joe put a science to it. He knows details like: "That team had a tough loss, but their point guard couldn't play that day," or "This situation reminds me of the 2012 bracket." His recollection of all the incidences over the years is remarkable. He's a true historian of the NCAA Tournament and the selection process. If you love college basketball like I do, you'll love reading about how Bracketology came to be and how it has become such an integral part of our game.

—Mark Few
Gonzaga University
men's basketball head coach

Introduction

M uch like I had been for the past dozen or so years, I was assigned to write a couple of articles for the official program of the 2019 Final Four. One of the assignments was to write about the creation and development of Bracketology, the art of predicting the field for the NCAA Men's Basketball Championship. As a college hoops nerd, I thought it might be fun to learn about the history of this sports phenomenon.

I had no idea.

The NCAA and its communications partner, IMG College, suggested that I reach out to Joe Lunardi, the guy who created it. I'd seen him on TV for the past several seasons, and he seemed like a nice enough guy. But you never know if his TV personality is *anything* like his real personality.

I found him to be funny in a self-deprecating way, articulate, confident, and humble at the same time. When we finished up our hour-long interview—about four times longer than I usually spent with an interview—I told him that I appreciated his humor and his humility. He responded, "Can you call my wife and tell her that?"

For the next couple of weeks, I kept mulling over the idea of approaching Joe with the idea of writing a book about the subject. It scared me a little because if it took an hour for me to interview him for a 1,500-word story, how long would it take to do the interviews for a book? But mostly, I thought about the fact that he was a national personality and I was, well, just me.

I finally had the courage to approach him with "another idea" related, yet unrelated, to the Final Four story, and he seemed interested. When we talked again, I said, "Have you ever considered writing a book about Bracketology?"

He said, "Yeah, I've been approached quite a few times." I asked him who had written it with him, and he said, "No one. I've never done it. I don't think anyone would care enough about the story to buy a book."

Challenge accepted.

I spent the next few months trying to convince him that it could be a big seller. Joe told his wife that another guy had approached him about a book on his "baby," and this time he was intrigued. Her reply was classic: "Isn't that more like a pamphlet?"

Joe's agent, Maury Gostfrand, was in my corner, and we finally convinced Joe to try it. He and I spent the next few months working on the project, doing so almost exclusively remotely, and we finished it during the 2020 pandemic. With the help of Triumph Books, I think we've got a winner. My wife, Tammy, and Joe's wife, Pam, will wait to see how many copies we sell, but as Joe's dad used to tell him, "Behind every successful man is a surprised woman."

I'm thrilled with how this book turned out and I've become very good friends with Joe through the process. And if you enjoy reading it half as much as I enjoyed helping him put it together, it will hold a valuable space on your bookcase for years to come.

—*David Smale*

CHAPTER ONE

The Greatest Tournament of All

The UCLA dynasty under John Wooden is overrated. It's *not* the greatest accomplishment in college basketball history. There, I said it. Bracketology can make you crazy that way.

Of course, seven straight NCAA titles—and 10 in a 12-year span—is a remarkable streak. But it needs context. Having to win only four games for all but one of their championships—two victories coming in the weakest region of a much smaller tournament field—made what the Bruins achieved considerably easier than it would be today.

Until Wooden's last title in 1975, which was a five-game journey, UCLA had a much easier road through the tournament than our current champions do. The Bruins never had to face teams from the ACC, the SEC, the Big Ten, or any of the storied independents, such as Notre Dame, until the very last game. Final Four matchups paired West versus Midwest until 1973. And there simply were fewer schools, particularly high-level basketball schools, west of the Mississippi.

Occasionally the Big Eight or the old Southwest Conference would have strong representatives, but the caliber and depth of play in those conferences wasn't as consistently good as that of the ACC or other leagues in the eastern time zone. In its run of championships between 1964 and 1975, UCLA often had a cakewalk to the Final Four. It's no coincidence that the only time the Bruins were bracketed against an ACC team prior to the title game, they lost to North Carolina State in the 1974 semifinals. The Bruins may have been on another planet in terms of talent, but often during their championship run, that talent was untested.

Obviously, those UCLA teams were great. If you're starting Lew Alcindor (later Kareem Abdul-Jabbar) or Bill Walton at center six times in an eight-year period, you're going to win a lot. But having to win six games in a deeper, balanced NCAA field—with the geographic wealth and dozens of quality at-large teams spread equally—is much harder than any path the Bruins faced during their glory years.

For a No. 1 seed today, even conceding a walk-over in the first round against a No. 16 seed—apologies to the University of Maryland, Baltimore County—a national championship typically requires a team to win at least four or five big-time games. For most of UCLA's run, the Bruins were getting by with only two or sometimes three high-level opponents. To the bracketologically-inclined, those things matter.

During the nine-year span of 1986 to 1994, Duke advanced to the Final Four seven times. From my seat and comparing the respective wins required, each of those appearances in the national semifinals is roughly equivalent to one of UCLA's national championships in the late 1960s and early 1970s. I'm not downplaying UCLA's run. I'm just saying it's not alone as an all-time achievement in the sport. Reaching a Final Four in today's expanded bracket—and the steadily increasing number of at-large bids makes the field *way* stronger—is far more impressive than you think.

The flip side is the level of talent overall, as well as its age and distribution. With Alcindor, Walton, Walt Hazzard, Gail Goodrich, Sidney Wicks, Curtis Rowe, and many others, UCLA was fantastic, assembling star-studded rosters seemingly without restriction and keeping them together year after year. Wooden's teams were much better than the top programs today—even if what they accomplished needs reframing.

Duke had the potential to be a generationally great team in 2018–19. Freshmen Zion Williamson, RJ Barrett, and Cam Reddish all were taken in the first 10 picks of the ensuing NBA draft. Yet the Blue Devils lost in the Elite Eight to Michigan State. And even had they cut down the nets, I would not compare them favorably to the best of the UCLA dynasty. Williamson as a freshman simply couldn't match Alcindor or Walton as upperclassmen. Since neither Alcindor nor Walton were permitted to play as freshmen, there's no way to make a completely fair comparison.

Yet even as we lean toward favoring UCLA's rosters in their run of titles, I maintain it is much harder to win an NCAA championship today.

Let's not forget how the tournament has evolved through the years, marking what I call the "modern era" with the advent of the 64-team bracket in 1985. We've been at the current 68-team composition since 2011, but that is a far cry from how the tourney looked at its founding.

From the first year of the championship in 1939 through 1950, there were only eight teams included. In 1951 and 1952, there were 16 teams, as college basketball grew in popularity. From 1953 through 1968, the field ranged from 22 to 25 teams, and seven to 10 byes were factored in each year. From 1969 to 1974, the field was fixed at 25 teams with seven byes, and UCLA never failed to receive one. The years 1975–1978 brought the onset of at-large bids— credit Maryland and Lefty Driesell, among others—with 32 teams invited and no byes. In 1979 the field expanded to 40 teams with 24 byes and still more at-large invites. The team tally trended upward in the early 1980s from 48 to 52 to 53 teams. The powers that be sought the right balance between automatic qualifiers and at-large participants.

The bracket gymnastics came to an end in 1985 when the field fully expanded to an aesthetically perfect 64 teams (no byes). Even with minor expansion to 65 teams from

2001 to 2010, featuring a single opening-round game, and to 68 in 2011 with the new look First Four, the tournament really gets going in the eyes of the public when the main bracket of 64 is set. Those who lose in the opening round still get to count those games as tournament appearances, but for the millions and millions of people filling out brackets, noon eastern of the middle Thursday of March is the true tipoff of the madness. And it must be purely coincidental just how many fans come down with a case of the sniffles at exactly that moment.

Besides the fewer number of teams in the field, why was it easier to win the NCAA title four or five decades ago? From its founding and through most of the next 45 years, the tournament was configured geographically. Teams in the western part of the U.S. were placed in the West Region. Teams from the Midwest were placed in the Midwest Region and so on. The nation's population dictated more schools and commensurate deserving teams being closer to the East Coast than there were in the western U.S.

For example, the one-time ECAC (East Coast Athletic Conference) wasn't a conference in today's terms. But as a critical scheduling alliance, including many high-profile members, the NCAA had to take it seriously. Forerunners to the current Men's Basketball Committee might have said, "We'd better take the team that has the best record in each of the ECAC divisions." The ones just on the wrong side of the not-yet-named "bubble" were invited to the still-highly regarded National Invitation Tournament (NIT).

For a generation or more, the West Region was considered the weakest. Look at some of UCLA's first-round opponents from 1964 through 1975: Seattle, Wyoming, New Mexico State, Long Beach State, Weber State. Which of those scare you? The Bruins' 10 title teams won these "contests" by an average of more than 20 points per game.

Interestingly, UCLA didn't make the NCAA Tournament in 1966 because only one team from a conference could participate, and the Bruins finished second to Oregon State in what was then known as the Pac-8. Of course, had freshmen been eligible that year, UCLA might very well have won 10 straight national championships. The freshman team at UCLA in 1966 included Alcindor, Lucius Allen, and Kenny Heitz, who would become crucial members of a championship nucleus beginning in 1967. In fact, those freshmen beat Wooden's varsity by 15 points—the two-time defending NCAA champions and preseason No. 1, mind you—in the first game ever played in Pauley Pavilion. But that's a story for a different book. A geography book, perhaps.

These days, the public pays almost as much attention to where a team is seeded, and where it plays, as to whether it's in or out of the field. Teams on the bubble probably look for their names first, but fans of most of the other teams search for their seed line and then compare themselves to other teams on that same line.

Speaking from experience and with an eye toward social media—something Wooden never had to think about—I get far more complaints about where I have a team seeded than about who I include or exclude. *How can you (fill-in-the-derogatory) make us a (fill-in-the-blank) seed? Don't you watch TV? We've beaten two teams you have seeded ahead of us.* The drumbeat of these and many other "suggestions" is never-ending, and I love it.

Prior to 1979 there was no seeding. Teams generally were placed in the region that most corresponded to their part of the country. The NCAA Men's Basketball Committee—commonly referred to as the Selection Committee—tried to match up teams in an economical way that made geographic sense. The notion of UCLA being a No. 1 seed and playing a No. 16 seed such as Florida International, an actual matchup for UCLA's 1995 title team, never would have happened in the Wooden era.

The pre-seeding era also had to contend with what has become a dinosaur in college sports: the major independent. There may have been a system in selecting said teams, but if your vision is one of good ol' boys making it up as they go along, you wouldn't be far from the truth. Not much was written down in terms of process, and there was little scrutiny of the outcomes.

There was plenty of tradition and plenty of room in the field for independents such as Marquette, DePaul, Notre Dame, and Villanova. Marquette won a national championship for Al McGuire in 1977, and Villanova lost to UCLA in the 1971 title game—both as independents. But the eventual anointing of at-large teams would make conference membership a must.

Similarly, the old way of selecting tournament participants was destined for failure. It may have met its demise with the 1974 ACC Tournament. The championship game pitted North Carolina State led by David Thompson, Tom Burleson, and a 5'7" point guard named Monte Towe against Maryland, featuring Tom McMillen, Len Elmore, and John Lucas. All of those players had NBA careers. Many have called that the greatest college basketball game ever played.

N.C. State won 103–100 in overtime. With the victory N.C. State went to the NCAA Tournament and ultimately ended UCLA's championship streak in the national semifinals. UCLA would come back and win one last title for Wooden in 1975, but the Wolfpack stopped the Bruins and Bill Walton with that dramatic 80–77 victory in double-overtime.

Many insist Maryland was the second best team in the country that year. It only lost five times. The Terrapins lost to UCLA in Los Angeles in the season opener. They lost at North Carolina in ACC play. And they lost three times to N.C. State, including the historic ACC Tournament final. Coached by the aforementioned Driesell, the Terps finished with a final Associated Press ranking of No. 4, but because of the rule that didn't allow more than one team from a conference to appear in the NCAA Tournament, Maryland watched from home.

That was also the last year of a 25-team bracket. How different would history have been had Maryland's historic season come a year later, when there were 32 NCAA teams, or two years later, when two teams from the same conference were allowed to participate? We saw the results of the latter change in its first iteration, when Indiana defeated Michigan—both from the Big Ten—in the 1976 national championship game in Philadelphia. Those Hoosiers are well remembered as the last team to win the championship with an undefeated record.

Beginning in 1980 the restriction on the number of teams from the same league was eliminated altogether. Today we regularly see major conferences get seven, eight, or nine teams in the tournament. A 16-member Big East set a record with 11 bids in 2011.

The introduction of the RPI (Rating Percentage Index) happened in 1981. The RPI was not just a tool for the selection and seeding process, but also a metric that frequently justified tournament consideration for teams with mediocre records. Who you played became as important, if not more important, than winning. The arithmetic of the RPI was simple and it contained three factors. A given team's winning percentage was the first component, counting 25 percent. Factor No. 2 was the winning percentage of that team's opponents—otherwise known as strength of schedule—and for two-plus decades, it was 50 percent of the formula. Factor No. 3 or the remaining 25 percent was your opponents' schedule strength.

More often than not, the RPI helped the rich get richer. Power conference members, who could rack up wins before league play, could take artificially gaudy records into their respective conference schedules. It became a rising tide lifting every boat in said leagues, and even losing teams ranked well in the eventual data seen by the Selection Committee.

Where the RPI did help was in balancing the field geographically. Without data it would be difficult, if not impossible, for the committee to produce a legitimate seed list that assigned a numeric value to every team in the field. Today with each team on the board ranked from 1 to 68, it is possible to compare regions (or segments of each region) to one another in terms of overall strength and quality. No longer will we have the days of the UCLA dynasty, when winning the West Region was easier because fewer high-end teams were slotted there. Since 1985 the top seeds in the West have included non-western schools such as St. John's (twice), Kentucky, Connecticut (twice), Cincinnati, Georgetown, Syracuse, Xavier, and even Duke.

Georgetown coach John Thompson reportedly asked to be sent to the West Region because he wanted to take his team away from any possible distractions. Intentional or not, "Hoya Paranoia" spent the 1984 tournament in Pullman, Washington; Los Angeles; and finally Seattle before Patrick Ewing and his teammates emerged with the national championship over Akeem Olajuwon and Houston's "Phi Slama Jama" squad.

Ultimately, the committee balanced regions in an effort to make them—top to bottom—as equal as possible. Georgetown was an exception in seeking its isolation. More common were complaints on the order of: "Why do we have to travel? Why do we have to go where our fans will have trouble following us?"

The committee has worked under multiple considerations over the years. The people try to avoid rematches of regular-season games. They try to avoid pairing two teams from the same conference too early in the tournament. These were some of the early guiding principles.

The great Maryland team of 1974 wouldn't miss the tournament today. A generation later the Terps would probably be a No. 1 seed—or at worst a No. 2 outside their natural geographic region. And they wouldn't have to face N.C. State a fourth time until the Final Four or at least the Elite Eight. Today's Men's Basketball Committee publishes these and other elements of its process in a document conveniently called the "Principles and Procedures for Selection, Seeding, and Bracketing." Most college basketball followers don't know it by that name. Instead they know it by "Bracketology."

* * *

No one knew how popular the concept of Bracketology would become, but the same principles developed by the committee for its work are necessary for the average fans—especially those with more than a pure rooting interest—as they fill out their brackets (for amusement only, of course).

Because the committee didn't have a detailed system—at least one that was somewhat public and/or discernable—Bracketology couldn't have happened before the 1980s. With a small number of at-large teams, the field was largely predetermined for the committee based on conference champions.

Another milestone was the emergence of ESPN in 1979, and the new network had a need for programming. College basketball was easy pickings, and the sport appeared all over the new network. That led to a generation of new fans and exposure to a host of quality teams across the country. "More and more people got into it, tracked it, followed it," said Greg Shaheen, the longtime NCAA staff liaison to the Selection Committee. "College basketball is unique because unlike college football and pro sports it has a saturated number of teams. We've long had more than 320 teams in the mix. Everybody has a school that they went to, or their neighbors went to, or their kids went to, or their grandparents went to. Often that school is just a few miles away from where they live. People have both a natural interest and a curiosity to understand how all this connects. College basketball was the beneficiary of that. The process needed to happen. I know the committee was mindful of how the process in general needed to come together. But the culture was such that it was truly cloaked in secrecy for the longest time, and the principles and procedures involved in assembling the bracket weren't publicized."

Shaheen joined the NCAA staff in 2000 and almost immediately was assigned to work with the Men's Basketball Committee. Shaheen was the visionary who said, "Why does this have to be a secret? If we share with people our *how*, they are much more likely to understand our *what*. We can still kind of keep closeted our *why*."

Shaheen was the outsider in the room, so he had a better understanding of what was being talked about out there versus what really happened on the inside. He pointed out that the need to inform the public and quite frankly to better inform the NCAA membership was a clear and obvious necessity. He also tried to convince the committee that the credibility of the NCAA was at stake. In the summer of 2001, he put together a proposal to have the committee start doing mock bracketing exercises *publicly*. He first wanted to do it with the press before ultimately engaging coaches, other constituencies in the sport, and the public in general.

For four years Shaheen proposed it, and the committee declined. Finally, in 2005 he put the proposal forward yet again, and it was approved. Shaheen's comment was simply, "What do we have to lose?" The annual rite of passage in guessing the proposal's margin of defeat was no more. "It was so clear that this was long overdue," he said. "It was helpful for everybody involved, including the staff and the committee ironically. So it was a major turning point in understanding the dialogue regarding the process."

Not everyone was going to agree with the committee's actual selections. Shaheen convinced them that that's okay. To the degree that they could be transparent, he convinced them to be transparent. "The process needed to be publicized," Shaheen said. "The rules and procedures were public, but most people didn't know they were public. Most people, who did know, generally treated them as unreadable. They couldn't understand them unless it was something they were doing full time. The need for structure and the need for understanding the structure really came about and coincided with the growth of the game."

People like me, essentially mimicking the work of the NCAA and literally explaining the process to the public, certainly moved those involved toward a more modern view. Most of the questions in the early years of Bracketology were process questions like: "Why were Villanova and Georgetown placed so far apart?" or "Why can't Kentucky and Louisville play closer to home?"

People didn't really understand that two schools in the old Big East couldn't play early in the tournament. The committee made no effort to explain even the most basic elements. Now most of those things are part of the common understanding and the common vernacular related to the buildup toward Selection Sunday. The questions I get today are much more nuanced. "How do you distinguish between Indiana and Iowa State if they're both 22–9 with a 12–6 league record in a Power Five conference and they haven't faced each other?" Once I established an ability to predict the brackets with increasing accuracy, the answers to those questions were immediately and urgently in demand among readers, viewers, coaches, players, media, and everyone else in college basketball. "Joe's approach to it is interesting because he studies what the outcome is in general," Shaheen he said. "He anticipates where he believes the committee is going to come from. It is valuable. Everybody involved in it—if they're going to do the process right—has to set their biases at the door. In order to best emulate where the bracket is going to come out, those who are really valued in terms of their perspective—and Joe is certainly lead among them—have to do the same. I think his game got better as we got more transparent because he was able to further tweak his understanding of the culture and the dynamics in the room. It really validated the fact that you have to do that. Impartiality is the only way you can do it."

It took 10 years after the field expanded to 64 teams to prepare my first public mock bracket. It's tempting to say I was smart enough to know Bracketology would become part of every sports fan's vocabulary. I could say that I was smart enough to know my work would lead to the creation of a small industry. I could even say that I was smart enough to know Selection Sunday would become the biggest non-sporting sporting event in our country. But I won't lie. I'm just an average Joe.

No matter how good the projections get, with all the formulas available, there will always be controversy. If similar teams are competing for the last spot in the field, any distinction is critical. Besides the formulas there are 10 different people with 10 different perspectives trying to reach a consensus. It's an inexact science.

I used to think there was no chance that my publicizing the process—and in some cases nailing the field completely—caused the committee to re-examine how they went about their business. I always assumed they had better things to do. They're athletic directors and conference administrators with real jobs the rest of the year. Maybe the swim team needed a new van. Who knows? But it's pretty obvious the level of scrutiny, which has been brought on in part because of people like me, has helped the overall process. The committee has been smart enough to realize that more information would bring about greater credibility and more interest. That all happened on Shaheen's watch.

And with Bracketology so popular, overt mistakes are not going to escape fan attention. In 2003 there was a fundamental bracketing error. The committee slotted Brigham Young into a region where—had the Cougars advanced to the Elite Eight—they would have had to play on a Sunday. BYU has a school rule—which the NCAA honors—prohibiting athletic competition on Sundays. The error wasn't discovered until after the bracket was revealed. The committee had to amend itself, saying to BYU, "If you advance, you're going to have to swap regions with somebody else." I was sitting in the ESPN studio as that year's brackets were being unveiled. Right away I said, "Uh, oh, they've got to fix that."

So it was determined before the tournament began that there would be regional checkers, if you will. If BYU made it out of the first weekend, its pod would be swapped with one from another region not ending on a Sunday. The point became moot when the Cougars lost in the first round to UConn. But imagine if BYU, a No. 12 seed, reached the Sweet 16 and was then shipped to another region. Some team would be awfully cranky about *not* facing a No. 12 when it was supposed to (and vice versa for whomever was shifted into BYU's spot). You know that team's opponent would have been more than a little upset.

Things are even more complicated when BYU is part of the First Four. The Cougars, who were twice sent to Dayton, Ohio, in recent years, can only play on the first Tuesday night of the tournament. Because if they played on Wednesday, they'd by definition be headed to a prohibited Friday/Sunday site for the first full weekend. It can really screw things up. In order to accommodate BYU, I also think the committee in the past has made the mistake of negatively impacting the seeding or placement of other teams. That is genuinely unfair and, I think, inarguable. I don't have anything against BYU's rule. The school is entitled to do and believe in whatever it wants. I respect BYU for standing by its principles. But that shouldn't negatively impact other schools that have chosen something different.

In other words, the only school whose seed should be changed in order to accommodate BYU should be BYU. Let's say this past season (the abbreviated 2019–20 campaign) that the natural landing spot for BYU would have been in San Jose, California, as a No. 7 seed. If that pod was a Friday/Sunday pod, the Cougars couldn't go there. So the committee would be forced to send BYU to a Thursday/Saturday location, say, in Albany, New York. Maybe the team that should otherwise have landed in Albany was Providence. Because BYU has to move, Providence has to go to San Jose. That doesn't seem fair to Providence. These things come up whenever the Cougars are in the field, as only half of the tournament sites are available to them. My solution would be to drop BYU's seed and minimize travel across the board. But at least we won't see the Cougars play bracket checkers again. The bracketing process is computerized now. If the committee tries to put BYU anywhere that feeds a Sunday site, BYU's name can't be entered on the screen. Consider this among many, many positive changes over the years.

What hasn't changed? The popularity of Bracketology. I, however, don't think the committee members look at my projected bracket as they're making their selections. It's tempting to say but quite misguided. I don't believe that has ever happened, at least not specifically. But we know committee members pay attention. Have they gone into that room—first in Kansas City, then Indianapolis, now New York—with every piece of paper and reference document they could get their hands on, including my seed list? Absolutely. I've had members tell me that.

The committee is sequestered, but I think it would be human nature to go in the opposite direction of my views if they happen to be on the fence about a particular team. If every time they take a break to watch games, there's a guy on TV saying they should do this, that, or the other thing, it's only human to go the other way. It's like parenting teenagers; sometimes the best way to get them to do something you want is to tell them to do the opposite.

There's also a likely groupthink dynamic going on. It's easy to feel insulated within a room of your peers. If somebody is advocating a position that may be more of an impulse in the short term than a good long-term review of a team's season, it's easy to see how that can take hold. If it's a powerful voice seconded by a couple of others who are well-respected, it's even more possible. That's probably the kind of thing that leads to the occasional head-scratcher. But not every slipup of the committee means they're acting in a political or malicious way. I think that any time you get 10 people in a room to debate anything, you're going to have a different outcome on Sunday than you had on Saturday, than you had on Friday, than you had on Thursday, etc.

Part of it is the fact that teams win and lose on those days, too. For some people those late results matter a great deal, but they don't matter as much to others. There is no written formula to account for that. These are smart people with the best of intentions. That makes it possible to get close to their thinking. I will brag a little and say that through the 2019 tournament I have missed zero or one team more than half the time in 20-plus years. In 2019 we had the correct seed for 60 teams. That's a pretty good record. And, tongue firmly in cheek, I'm confident I would have nailed the entire 2020 bracket, including every seed and destination of all 68 teams had the 2020 tournament not been cancelled three days before the bracket was set to be announced.

But the single greatest impact of Bracketology hasn't been getting the committee to pick or seed a team or a league in a certain way. I don't think my advocacy has any influence there. But the level of exposure, the level of scrutiny that did not exist at all before 1995 has forced the committee to up its game significantly. I will gladly take credit for that.

Much of the bragging about this or that school reaching the NCAA Tournament every year borders on the ridiculous. The way the system is now it's almost impossible for the top programs to miss it.

First of all, in the non-conference portion of the season, those teams play few if any true road games. Duke, for example, will play a true non-conference away game every other year in the ACC/Big Ten Challenge. All their other non-league games are either at home or on a neutral court. The Blue Devils, of course, are playing incredibly high-level games. They're playing in a loaded Maui Invitational every four years. They're going to the Preseason NIT in Madison Square Garden. They're not playing local Division II schools. But the hardest game to win in college basketball is the road game. We know that because home teams win more than 70 percent of the time. It's an established fact of life in Division I. I tend to judge programs more by year-over-year seeding. The fact that Kansas has made the NCAAs every year since missing the 1989 tournament (and that was due to probation) is not what's impressive. It's the fact that they've been a top four seed 28 times in those 30 years.

Virginia's epic first-round loss to UMBC in 2018—when it became the first No. 1 seed to lose to a No. 16 seed—was the biggest aberration. The Cavaliers were criticized as being the ultimate underachievers. They got the monkey off their back a year later when they won the national championship in a classic overtime game against Texas Tech. With that victory the negative labels vanished. But the Cavaliers should never have been labeled in the first place. In a five-year period, in which Virginia had been a No. 1 seed three times, there was nothing underachieving about their run. The Cavaliers won the most games in college basketball during that span. They didn't win the very last game until 2019. But that doesn't make them any less good.

You could argue that being a No. 1 seed is even more difficult than reaching the Final Four. It requires three months of being great, as opposed to three weeks. Kansas was a No. 1 seed eight times between 2007 and 2018, but the Jayhawks won only one national championship. I've said— and I've gotten a lot of criticism for it—that the Jayhawks are the "Atlanta Braves of college basketball." The Braves won 14 straight National League East Division titles from 1991 to 2005 (there was no division winner in 1994 because of the Major League Baseball players' strike). But they won the World Series just once (in 1995).

Did Kansas underachieve because it only has one title in this era like the Braves? Or has Kansas just been consistently superior? Shouldn't we just tip our hats and ignore a little bit of bad luck against teams like Bucknell and Northern Iowa? It doesn't matter what my opinion is. Because if you're a Kansas fan, you're going to think the Jayhawks underachieved. Such debates are one of the primary reasons college basketball is great. And for me, trying to pick the NCAA Tournament field is the greatest debate of all.

CHAPTER TWO

*The Birth
of Bracketology*

L ike a lot of good things, Bracketology was an accident. I was fortunate to be an editor for the *Blue Ribbon College Basketball Yearbook* in the early 1990s, when *Blue Ribbon* was considered the bible of college basketball. It had in-depth write-ups of all the Division I men's basketball teams in the country. It wasn't like other preview magazines that had just a thumbnail of most teams and often featured outdated information.

Blue Ribbon was more like a phone book. Its subscribers comprised a who's who of the sport. It was founded in 1981 in tiny Buckhannon, West Virginia, by a young hoops junkie named Chris Wallace, who leaned on family and friends to type up reams and reams of coffee-stained copy. On his way to becoming an NBA general manager—first with the Boston Celtics and recently the Memphis Grizzlies—Wallace hired an even younger hoops junkie named Joe Lunardi to write up the Ivy League team previews one summer.

I was part of a group, including current *Blue Ribbon* publisher Chris Dortch, who bought the book from Wallace when he moved up to the NBA. We only had one meeting—in Knoxville, Tennessee, after a Sunday afternoon

Tennessee–Florida game in January 1994—and the shortest guy at the table also had the biggest mouth (you know who that is) and he wouldn't let go of the idea of adding an NCAA Tournament preview edition to the *Blue Ribbon* lineup.

The idea was to bring the singular *Blue Ribbon* treatment to March Madness. We would work all through Selection Weekend, go to print on Sunday night after the NCAA field was announced, and then ship an 80-page book to subscribers in time for them to digest our analysis and fill out brackets ahead of Thursday afternoon's tip-off. Not surprisingly, the first 500 copies we sold went to an address in Las Vegas.

Also remember this was the infancy of the Internet when far less information was available to the general public. We filled the void with stats, trends, and in-depth coverage of every team's strengths and weaknesses. We threw in a few predictions, many of which made us look smarter than we were, and managed not to lose our shirts on printing and shipping costs.

With my new buddy, Dortch, handling the business side from his home in Chattanooga, Tennessee, and the legendary-in-basketball-camp-circles Diane Swiger taking orders in Buckhannon, I ran the editorial operation in Philadelphia. It was the original bracket bunker. A half-dozen die-hards herded correspondents at every conference tournament in the country. No cell phones, no Internet, but we had an overworked fax machine and one dial-up modem.

There would be no such thing as Bracketology if not for those bunker weekends at my Saint Joseph's University office. Staying awake 50 straight hours every year was a testament to late-night cheesesteaks and morning coffee infusions from longtime St. Joe's athletic director Don DiJulia, whose insights and inspiration are invaluable to this day. Those writers and editors birthed a phenomenon, a fact that didn't sink in until we saw Jim Nantz sitting at the CBS anchor desk three days later with a copy of our book at his side.

There was only one problem. The editor—the same little guy with the big nose and big mouth—didn't know what he was doing. Oh, I knew basketball well enough, but I didn't know anything about business. You know, apparently, it's a good thing for revenue to exceed expenses. Bottom line: the launch of *Blue Ribbon's* tournament preview was an editorial success and a financial non-entity. We made enough to cover the cheesesteaks and not much more. We were having a ball but working far too hard for too little gain.

With a print deadline of midnight Sunday, less than six hours after the Selection Show, we were in a bind. Not knowing who would make the field and where, we had to prepare write-ups for way more than the 64 teams that would be selected. Once the bracket came out, we had to be ready to "plug and play." We then realized we could make our jobs easier—and save a whole lot of overhead—if we had a more exact sense of who those 64 teams would be. As the nerd on staff, I started studying the selection process to cut down the number of required previews. It had nothing to do with what we now know as Bracketology.

That name came a few years later. *The Philadelphia Inquirer* reporter Mike Jensen was writing an article about Temple's tournament chances that season. He quoted me as "a local bracketologist," which I suppose is one step up from neighborhood proctologist (or worse). So, while I would like to take all of the credit for the growth of my new field, it was more a matter of being in the right place at the right time. Jensen, however, says it was me who came up with the term. He sent me the aforementioned article, and it says, "Lunardi, who calls himself a 'bracketologist.'" He said recently, "Joe may think I came up with it, but I am *sure* Joe came up with it."

Whichever the case, Bracketology followed "bracketologist," and away we went. The label was perfect from the start, but it took off after ESPN.com was created and added my in-season projections to the college basketball content menu. The projections were primarily a means to promote *Blue Ribbon*—not the other way around. I actually remember the day Bracketology became a thing. On January 7, 2002, Bracketology got its own page in ESPN. com's college basketball section. For the first time, the projections were more than line-by-line text on a plain HTML page. ESPN had added graphics, a visual bracket, and links from each team in the field to its pertinent tournament information. ESPN linked to its new creation from the front page of the site. I remember there being something like a quarter-million page views in an hour and a half. The college basketball editor at the time, Ron Buck, called me and said, "Everybody in the newsroom is going like 'Holy you-know-what.'"

My response was on the order of, "That sounds good. Is it?" I wasn't smart enough to quip or ask, "Can I get paid by the click?" Within six weeks the web traffic led an emerging ESPNews channel to use me as part of its studio coverage of the tournament. Until that point I'd never been on TV for basketball.

When the 2002 tournament ended and I made my last trip home from ESPN headquarters in Connecticut, it was hard not to think that I was pretty close to being in the mainstream. The next challenge would be to make Bracketology better—more accurate, more interesting, more compelling. At no point was I thinking about becoming

"Joey Brackets." I had a real job—not to mention a young family—and was still involved peripherally as a contributor to *Blue Ribbon*.

No one had any idea Bracketology would become an annual obsession. And it's not too far off to say it's so much fun that I would do it for nothing. (After all, in the early years, I was doing it for mostly nothing.) But there really is a market for good information, and my family certainly prefers that I not provide it free of charge.

The early years were challenging because of my own lack of experience and the fact that information to predict the field better wasn't easily available. Most of my mistakes in those days were procedural things or errors in data. Many of those tasks have since been automated. It also took some time to gain confidence in my analytical abilities, particularly with teams near the bubble. I would question myself. I also was more easily influenced by feedback that countered my own evaluations. After all, who was I to disagree with the legends of the game at ESPN or across the country?

Eventually, to quote my hometown Philadelphia 76ers, I learned to trust the process. Most years, even in the inevitable circumstances when the Selection Committee throws a curveball or two, I'm confident enough to believe that each and every bracket is sound. I believe the committee's procedures have been applied neutrally and consistently. And, most importantly, I believe that reasonable people can disagree without either being in error—especially when you get down to the last handful of teams.

* * *

In 2003–04 Air Force won the Mountain West regular season by two full games. The Falcons weren't a particularly powerful team, but the committee's history up to that point was to award at-large bids if needed to conference champions of multi-bid leagues. Because of that I had Air Force in the field. I happened to be walking into one of the ESPN studios to do a segment during Championship Week. The primary on-air talent for that particular show was the legendary Richard "Digger" Phelps. The former Notre Dame coach downplayed the chances of Air Force reaching the tournament that year. "There's no way Air Force is going to make it," he said. "I've seen them. They're not very good. Anybody who has seen them would believe that."

For better or worse, I got nervous and took them out of my next bracket. This caused outrage from Falcons fans everywhere, who questioned everything from my basketball judgment to my love of country and specifically the U.S. Air Force Academy. (Actually, my father was an Army Air Corps bomber pilot with 50 mission credits in World War II.)

Back in the hotel that night, I pulled out my handy-dandy NCAA Tournament record book, dog-eared pages and all, and started looking for precedent to better evaluate the Falcons. They were the outright winners of a multi-bid league, which meant they were a tournament team. Not because I said so or another analyst said so but because the committee had said so every year up to that point. One day after taking them out, I reversed course and put them back in. I thought, *No offense, but what does Digger know? Does he have year-by-year bid sheets in front of him? Has he studied every set of selections for 20 years?*

It didn't appease the people who were mad at me; it just made them less frustrated. But I did offend another team's fans because the Falcons' re-inclusion took someone else out of the field. It was a crude reminder that at any given time—with the number of Division I teams reaching 357—that fans from at least 289 schools are going to think I'm nuts. In the end Bracketology case law prevailed. Air Force made the field in 2004. They returned to the bracket just two years later in what turned out to be an even more controversial decision by the committee.

In 2006 Air Force got in with a substandard at-large resume. There wasn't much precedent in its favor in terms of teams with comparable profiles. Plus the Falcons were upset in the first round of their conference tournament. The

Falcons got by on account of the dreaded eye test. A few people in the committee room apparently felt Air Force belonged because it utilized a Princeton-style offense that made it hard to play against. I believe the following as clearly as the sun is high: the reason to include or exclude teams from the NCAA Tournament isn't because they play slow or they play fast, because they milk the clock or shoot threes, because they have a high-post center or a left-handed point guard. I came to realize that the eye test, at least in ways pertaining to tournament selections, is mostly a load of crap.

No disrespect to coaches and former coaches, scouts, or other basketball people who chart every X and O from Maine to Hawaii, who know the percentage of possessions a given team blitzes the high ball screen, who think such and such is great because they have two potential draft picks, and so on. Who cares? With the rarest of exceptions, the NCAA selection process has to be results based. Did you win enough games? Try this analogy from another sport. In baseball would you rather have a fat guy who hits or a Ted Williams replica who can't get the ball out of the infield? Give me John Kruk—the stereotypical fat guy—any day of the week. In our sport the question isn't whether a team has two lottery picks. It's whether that team wins enough because of it.

When I differ with the committee, it's usually over the fine print. Most of the time I can honestly say, "I understand what they were thinking." I've even had former committee members say the same thing to and about me. Of course, there are times the committee is just picking the flavor of the month or falling for some kind of impulse criteria that doesn't hold up over time. This is when I spend the latter part of March in a snit. Then another season comes around, and all is right with the world.

I'm not going to lie. The thought of being known for creating something as popular as Bracketology is pretty cool. A few years ago the word made it into the *Oxford English Dictionary*, but I don't think that will fit on my tombstone. There are too many letters! When I talk to school groups, I like to tell them that when I was their age I was the nerd who was too small to play. Coaches would hand me a clipboard to keep track of some stats. I also was involved in speech and debate. So I learned how to communicate properly. A lot of this began at Damien High School in Southern California, where we lived for three years on account of my dad's job. In a way, all I'm doing today is an extension of what began at Damien. Sports and stats, speaking and persuading. Now I just have a bigger stage with more well-known topics.

And I still follow all other sports as a fan, hopefully applying some discipline to it and communicating certain points of view in an interesting and compelling way. Bracketology is not and was never meant to be some life-altering discipline. We're not saving lives in that Bracket Bunker. It's entertainment. A lot of people forget the "E" in ESPN actually stands for entertainment. I firmly believe you can take your work seriously without taking yourself seriously. I tell kids to find their passion, and that anyone can rise to the top of their field if he or she is willing to work at it.

The really funny thing is that I'm not an expert, in any way, shape, or form on the finer points of basketball. I've come up with ways to predict the NCAA Tournament field with a fair amount of accuracy, but I can't draw up an inbounds play (not a good one, anyway). I've been asked more times than I can count if there's a secret formula for coming up with the brackets, but there are no secrets to give away. I didn't invent the RPI, the NET rankings, KenPom, Sagarin, or any of the rating systems that have been used by the committee through the years. In the early days, I tried to read the tea leaves of the committee, trying to figure out which of the various criteria they would feel were the most important. Usually it was (RPI) Rating Percentage Index and (SOS) Strength of Schedule as opposed to the weekly media and coaches' polls that most fans would read in the newspapers. Fans might think they had the inside skinny with ratings like Jeff Sagarin's. Valuable as those ratings may have been, the committee's process was very different.

From the beginning my job was to replicate that process and not interject my own opinion. I found a lot of times in the early years that I would lag behind the committee. The results of one year's bracket might indicate a shift in their emphasis, so I would weigh things differently the following year. But what the committee considered important varied from season to season and team to team. There also are some very important differences between my role and that of the hundreds of terrific game and studio analysts on the air every night of the season. They say what they think *should* happen in terms of tournament selection and seeding. My job is to say what *will* happen based on the committee's process and practices.

Understand that my brackets carry very little personal opinion on the quality of the teams under consideration. I'm estimating what I think the committee is going to do. Those 10 individuals have the only votes that matter. My best skill—and maybe something that separates me from the others in this line of work—is collecting and aggregating data. You remember the scene near the end of *The Wizard of Oz*, where the wizard is behind the curtain, pulling on levers, and creating the smoke and loud noises? That's how I feel at times with my mixing board of data points, team-specific ingredients, and extensive personal observation. From year to year and often within the same season, I'll cut back on some ingredients and add a few others. A spoonful of sugar here, a little more spice there. Sometimes it works, and sometimes the cake falls flat before it gets out of the oven. Ultimately, Bracketology is as much art as science.

Given the amount of time spent on it, I'd like to think I'm as well-informed as anyone on the planet when it comes to the NCAA field. But it's not up to me who gets in. I'm a pundit, not a voter. Whether or not any of the 10 people who matter pay attention to what I think will always be a mystery. And if the committee was actually influenced by my brackets, Saint Joseph's University—my alma mater and former employer for more than 30 years—would never miss the tournament. Heck, I'd have the Hawks as a No. 1 seed every year.

But the truth is that my credibility is based on accuracy and neutral evaluations. There are even what I like to call hidden bias triggers built into the calculations. I've often said I'd put my own mother in the NIT if she played a soft schedule. But we're all human. Like you, I watch a lot of games. I like some teams, coaches, and players more than others and I root for the teams and coaches that I like. So maybe, even if I wanted to sneak Mom into the field as an 11-seed, the public would see right through any inconsistent evaluations.

I know my role. As a native of Philadelphia, I rooted for the Eagles to beat the New England Patriots in Super

Bowl LII. But there's no way, if there was an NFL playoff selection committee, that New England wouldn't have been the No. 1 overall seed that year. If I inject too much personal opinion, it's going to come through loud and clear. People would say that I don't know what I'm doing (even more than they do already). But it's my job to step back and be "the paper of record" in respect to who will be named on Selection Sunday. I feel like I'm accountable to a higher authority. I can't be a Republican or a Democrat. I have to play it right down the middle or the whole thing crumbles.

Part of what makes my version of Bracketology unique is that my work is not just on the Internet. During February and the first part of March, I'm a regular contributor on ESPN's studio shows, giving updates with every upset. Nearly a decade ago, I told the upper-level brass at ESPN that I could be a little more accurate if I wasn't sitting around the studio waiting for the next appearance on live TV. They very politely said, "We appreciate that you think that. But you being here, giving updates as things change, is great television. That's what people want, and we're here to serve the fans."

I realized at that moment that my business model was changing. I wasn't like the other guys anymore. Someday I'll step away, and somebody younger and smarter will take over. I hope they'll realize and appreciate, as I have, just how much fun it really is. Mindful that it's not life and death and that my predictions are about a basketball tournament, there's still a fair amount of pressure. I've picked all the teams correctly a handful of times with fields of 64, 65, and 68 teams. Generally speaking, I miss between one or two teams each year. Like a coach, I remember the few misses more than the multiple hits. In quiet moments sometimes I'll say to myself, *I can see what the committee saw there*. Other times, I'll say, *I don't think the committee looked at the data correctly*. But the committee is made up of humans. The truth is: if you're looking at the last few teams on the board, they all have warts.

I'm flattered by others trying to imitate me. In fact, many of them are better at the analytics part. But my position of being first and having the biggest platform is different. Also, the others don't have to give updates in real time every moment of every day during the last month of the season. That's certainly been the biggest change in my professional life. I'm friends with many of the others who have joined in the fun of predicting the NCAA Tournament brackets. We might email or text back and forth a little bit. But once the Super Bowl comes and goes and I head to Bristol, Connecticut, and the bunker for four or five weeks, I don't really talk much with anybody, including the people I'm related to. If I do communicate, it's more social, and there's not a lot of time for that. We might talk about what we think of a certain team, but I'm just too isolated in my world.

I don't mean to sound arrogant, but I know what I'm doing. If I listened to people outside that process, it's noise. I'm just better off doing my own thing. I don't communicate regularly with committee members either, though it does happen throughout the earlier portions of the season. They attend a lot of games. I attend a lot of games. But the conversations are pretty general in nature. There were some conversations with committee members leading up to the 2019 selections that went along the lines of me saying: "You've always been consistent with the final at-larges, especially when a team's non-conference schedule was indefensible. Do you see anything that would change that way of thinking?"

The conversation was regarding North Carolina State, which was in the middle of the ACC race and ended up at .500 in the league. But the Wolfpack finished with the No. 353 non-conference strength of schedule...out of 353 teams that season and did indeed miss the tournament. I had those conversations because I could see the fork in the road. I wanted to be on the right side of the decision. I also wanted the committee to remain consistent. To allow an at-large team to be almost entirely untested outside its conference would be very damaging to the sport, but I wasn't sure until the Selection Show that the committee would agree.

There have been times when I've gotten the top two or three lines dead on with location and seeding. Once you miss one team or site, though, the dominoes start to fall in every region. I've come to judge my own work more by seeding than the number of correct selections or their geographic placement. Bracketing rules are fixed, and the pairings are nearly impossible to manipulate. When I build a seed list, I completely disregard those things that don't impact the committee's selections. I do it every night for five months. I'm not bragging, I'm not even saying that's sane human behavior, I'm just saying that's what I do. Why? Because I will get calls at any time between the beginning of January and Selection Sunday afternoon, asking, "Who are your top seeds and who's on the bubble?"

I might get a call from the production truck in Manhattan, Kansas, getting ready for Kansas State hosting Oklahoma State. I get similar calls from every other region of the country. ESPN production folks see that their games involve a bubble team or two and they want to frame the discussion properly. One time about 15 years ago, I got a call from Brent Musburger. He was getting ready to go on the air with Illinois at Wisconsin. I thought it was one of my buddies needling me. He said, "This is Brent Musburger." I said, "Yeah, and I'm Brad Pitt" and then I hung up. Ten minutes later the phone rang again, and the voice said, "Joe, this *really is* Brent Musburger."

Nowadays, I make sure to always answer the phone with an open mind. Bracketology has made it so I never know who's on the line.

CHAPTER THREE

ESPN and College Basketball

ESPN was founded in 1979. It first appeared on the air on September 7 of that year when anchor George Grande welcomed viewers to a new concept: 24-hour sports television. It probably wasn't the first time somebody had thought of that idea. In fact, most sports fans probably thought about how great it would be to have sports on the air all the time. But nobody had done it before.

ESPN came into being at a time when college sports television—at least on the national level—meant one Saturday football game each week on ABC and one weekly basketball broadcast on NBC. There were regional weekend games like the ECAC Game of the Week in Philadelphia (featuring yours truly on stats) and ACC broadcasts up and down Tobacco Road, but the only weeknight college basketball I remember from the 1970s involved Notre Dame, and that was because of the school's national appeal. I remember Harry Kalas, the legendary Philadelphia Phillies broadcaster, doing those games every winter. I remember players like Kelly Tripucka, John Paxson, and Adrian Dantley, and, of course, head coach Digger Phelps. In the fall we also had Notre Dame football replays on Sunday mornings, featuring Lindsey Nelson.

When ESPN took to the airwaves, its initial programming included studio shows and whatever hadn't found a niche elsewhere. ESPN's founders probably knew at some level that college sports, especially college basketball, *could* grow exponentially, but what they stumbled into was pretty much an accident of circumstance. Negotiations with the NCAA were critical. ESPN was looking for any and all programming, and college sports were a great target. But if the first wave had been lawn bowling, we might all be following that instead of "Big Monday." A confluence of opportunity and available programming inventory, ESPN and college basketball were perfect together.

Think about college sports and particularly the programming genius behind college basketball. The biggest windows of time available for live sporting events were generally weeknights. National sports telecasts simply did not exist in those windows outside of *Monday Night Football*. *MNF* was revolutionary not because of the "Football" but because of the words "Monday" and "Night."

We got night games in the World Series, but that was only for a week or so and even that didn't start until the mid-1970s. There certainly weren't weeknight national broadcasts of college sports. You had four or five months sitting empty on the calendar with basically no national competition.

It took some intelligence and foresight to recognize the true value that college sports could bring. There were plenty of people who told the founders of ESPN that a 24-hour sports network was foolhardy. But ESPN saw something nobody else did, or at least recognized it like no one else. Every big city had regional sports. In Philadelphia I could watch the NBA's 76ers and the NHL's Flyers. Even then it was only the road games because the home games were blacked out. But there were a ton of weeknights the average sports fan could not watch sports, something that is inconceivable today.

Forty years later, the notion of going an entire week without being able to watch live sports would be ludicrous. Witness the spring and early summer of 2020 when no live sports took place in America because of the coronavirus. That was the first time our country had seen weeknights without sports since ESPN first came on the air. Half of our population has never had to live without seven-day-per-week live sports. Having since gone through sudden and total withdrawal, people have again proved they would watch pretty much anything. The ESPN revolution was real.

The eyeballs of potential sports fans were most available outside of baseball season and on weeknights, even though no over-the-air networks recognized it. The viewership of Australian Rules Football, tractor pulls, and other semi-sporting events proved that fans were hungry for live programming. What sport plays on weeknights in the fall and winter more than college basketball? ESPN was not getting the NBA at that point. It wasn't getting Major League Baseball or even the NHL. College basketball presented a combination of relatively inexpensive programming with the largest potential audience.

Because nearly every great college rivalry was a two-game series with a home game at each campus, there was typically at least one weeknight game in each series. The major networks weren't interested in the weeknight broadcasts, which made them available for the likes of ESPN. The biggest obstacle was syndication. Regional networks like Raycom had exclusive rights in particular areas, and in some cases, ESPN picked up those broadcasts and re-aired them to the rest of the country. They had no control over the day and time the games were played, but once the network gained traction, that changed. It begs the question: did college sports, especially college basketball, grow because of ESPN, or did ESPN grow because of college hoops? I think both can be true. To me there are three seminal occurrences that really led to the current popularity of college basketball.

The first would have occurred mostly in the 1960s, when the big state schools—the major college football powers, if you will—realized they could also make money at basketball.

For most of them, there had previously been only two seasons: football and spring football. Only a handful of Division I institutions—Kentucky, Indiana, and Kansas in the middle of the country and also UCLA, Duke, and North Carolina on the coasts—previously saw college basketball as a major enterprise.

If you look at the list of NCAA champions in the 1940s and 1950s, there are a lot of winners like Holy Cross, San Francisco, and La Salle. A little later came Loyola Chicago and Marquette. The sport was dominated primarily by urban, private, Catholic institutions. They certainly got their share and then some. And while there are still schools that can advance in the NCAA Tournament without being in Power Five football conferences—think Villanova, Gonzaga, and Butler in recent years—they are the exception now instead of the norm.

Once the big boys realized there was something to this roundball thing, they started to put more time, money, and energy into it, and the corresponding share of success shifted. Those schools were able to apply a huge advantage in resources. Had they chosen to put said resources into, say, water polo, that might have been just as successful. But basketball was the obvious niche to be explored and exploited.

A generation after that gradual shift, ESPN was born. In terms of picking low-hanging fruit as cheap, yet popular programming, college sports were a perfect match. They had a built-in audience because everybody attended school somewhere or knew somebody who did. Often that college was nearby, so there was a geographic connection. The expenses were modest, too, because the talent—the athletes themselves—was uncompensated. That gave a fledgling sports network a toehold in live events.

You also had a visionary in Dave Gavitt, who saw the potential to build an enterprise focused on college basketball and supported by television. The Big East Conference wasn't just based on geography, though its early members were all pretty much East Coast teams. It was based on television markets. It was built to deliver the largest audiences to that little box in the corner of your living room. Coincidentally, the Big East was launched in the same year as ESPN. The timing was perfect. The landmark 1979 NCAA men's basketball title game had been played less than six months prior to ESPN's debut. The championship matchup between Earvin "Magic" Johnson and Michigan State versus Larry Bird and Indiana State remains college basketball's highest-rated game of all time. When Dick Vitale made his debut on ESPN that December, there was a huge new fanbase anxious for more.

It seems so obvious now with 40-plus years of hindsight, but college basketball was arguably the most popular of the under-exposed sports. It literally was—from a sports perspective—America's best-kept secret. It had a regional following. Prior to 1979 the Final Four was probably the television equivalent of a mid-level bowl game. It wasn't the Rose Bowl or the Orange Bowl. It was more like the Gator Bowl or the Bluebonnet Bowl in terms of exposure and ratings.

The NCAA championship was still desired, but it hadn't been long since winning the NIT was just as big—if not bigger—than winning the NCAA Tournament. The final hurdle for eclipsing the prestige of the NIT occurred when the NCAA allowed multiple teams from a conference to participate in the 1975 tourney. With that change the NCAA also required that conference champions always choose its tournament over the NIT.

The scope of coverage provided by ESPN gave college basketball another entry into the mainstream, and it wasn't long before college basketball was on a path to "Big Monday" and beyond. Leading the way were weekly Big East games from the Carrier Dome, Boston Garden, Madison Square Garden, the Capital Center, and the Spectrum. The large and/or pro arenas gave national legitimacy to the programs calling them home. It brought to light new traditions and rivalries that were truly made for television.

Another huge break for fans—as well as ESPN—was getting the contract to broadcast the early rounds of the

NCAA Tournament. They were never televised until ESPN came around. And there are still people who long for those early ESPN days with cut-ins of so many great finishes. I know others who stayed up all night watching tape-delayed broadcasts of tournament games from earlier in the day.

I remember a late night in 1983, watching North Carolina State play Pepperdine in the opening round from Corvallis, Oregon. N.C. State had to make a late comeback to win in overtime 69–67. Two weeks later they were at "The Pit" in Albuquerque with Jim Valvano running around the court looking for someone to hug. Without ESPN a large part of the story is missing. It was all so fresh and new...and compelling. Today every game is on from start to finish across four different networks. You can put them on your screen like a tic-tac-toe board if you want or set up four screens together and not miss anything. That certainly was not the case before 1979.

There are a lot of people who had a huge influence on the growth of college basketball on ESPN and elsewhere, including Gavitt, who founded the Big East. But Gavitt was behind the scenes to the casual fan. There were others who were in front of the camera. That brings me to my fellow paisan, Vitale. In the early years of ESPN's coverage, he was the sport's cheerleader and unofficial PR man. Contrary to his critics at the time, I don't believe it was an act. Vitale genuinely loved—and still loves—college basketball. He was and is just so happy to be at a basketball game. The thought of getting paid to talk about it only adds to his good fortune. To this day, more than a thousand games later, Vitale says the same thing. As a coach he was good enough at the University of Detroit to get an NBA head job with the Detroit Pistons. Heck, he went to the semifinals of the Mideast Region in the 1977 NCAA Tournament. He was doing something right.

But Vitale wasn't chosen for the ESPN role at the time because of his big name. He was chosen because he was available, affordable, and had the energy and knowledge of the sport. He drew fans who may not have been hard-core, but they tuned in to see and hear what he would come up with next. In a way Vitale did for college basketball what Howard Cosell did for *Monday Night Football* but without the arrogance or the personal edge. Let's be honest: because of its youthful nature, the college basketball environment is one of optimism. Vitale's personality plays to that. I never met Cosell, but as many people probably tuned in to his broadcasts because they *didn't* like him as those who did.

In Dickie V's formative years, some people thought he was all schtick and not much substance. But if you listen—as those of us in college basketball have for 40-plus years—he really breaks down a game. And he makes it fun. Getting to know him personally, I've come to realize how genuine he is. If you run into Vitale at an airport or an arena or a restaurant, you get the same "Dickie V" that you get at a Duke–Carolina game. He's as approachable in person as he comes across on television. He's just so thrilled to be involved in college basketball. Others like Dick Enberg, Billy Packer, and Al McGuire also had a large role in the growth of college basketball because they did the weekly national game long before ESPN. They also called the biggest games of the NCAA Tournament for NBC through 1981.

And don't forget about the UCLA dynasty. Although I may have minimized the accomplishments of that era, there is no mistaking the Bruins' importance in the history of the sport. They were star-studded. They were the Yankees, the Celtics, or the Canadiens. Had the UCLA dynasty occurred in some small college town instead of Hollywood, it wouldn't have impacted the sport to the same degree.

* * *

You've probably never heard of Tom Odjakjian, ESPN's director of college sports from 1981 to 1994. But you could make a legitimate case that he is the forefather of Bracketology. Odjakjian saw the value in playing matchmaker for television. He had a way of framing the content—the games—to build storylines throughout the season. Odjakjian saw college basketball programming as a way to grow both the sport and the network. Unlike major college football, Division I basketball truly was a national sport. There's a Division I team in every state except Alaska, and ESPN tried to do big games from as many different states as possible. If the network televised Idaho vs. Boise State, for instance, it might not be a big ratings grab across the whole country. But it was a reason for sports fans in Idaho to add ESPN to their cable package. Odjakjian & Co. were also creative. One famous matchup was George Washington University vs. James Madison University on Presidents' Day. As you can imagine, ESPN got plenty of press for that one.

Another lynchpin for programming were the compelling coaching personalities. College basketball was and still is about the coaches. Coaches last at the top programs unlike their often one-and-done stars. You had "good guys" like John Wooden and Dean Smith and "villains" like Bob Knight and Jerry Tarkanian. ESPN and the Big East made legends out of Rollie Massimino, Lou Carnesecca, "Big John" Thompson, and Jim Boeheim. In another generation those coaches would not have been as well-known. They'd be like Jack Hartman, who was a great coach at Southern Illinois and later at Kansas State. He won more than two-thirds of his games and coached legends like Walt Frazier and Rolando Blackman. But Hartman wasn't a household name outside his region. People in the Midwest still talk about the characters among the coaches of the old Big 8 such as Billy Tubbs (Oklahoma), Johnny Orr (Iowa State), Norm Stewart (Missouri), and Hartman.

ESPN would have made them celebrities. Other coaches got their Hall of Fame monikers from Dick Vitale like "Robert Montgomery" Knight and "Michelangelo" Dean Smith. "Coach K" (Mike Krzyzewski) should probably give half his salary to Vitale. The two men weren't in business together per se, but in a way they were. There were plenty of other coaches whose personalities helped grow the game.

I think of two in particular: John Chaney of Temple and John Calipari of UMass. Those two guys realized television exposure was essential to lift their programs to be able to compete with the big boys. Temple joined the Atlantic 10 in its first year under Chaney (1982–83). Temple had reached the NCAA Tournament eight times between 1939 and 1982, but Chaney led the Owls to the NCAA Tournament 17 times in 18 years, beginning with his second season.

Before Calipari got there in the fall of 1988, UMass had not had a winning season in 10 years and had reached the NCAA Tournament only once in its history (1962). After going 10–18 in Calipari's first season, UMass reached the NIT the next two years, including the semifinals in his third season. Then he reached the NCAA Tournament five straight times, including the Elite Eight in 1995 and the Final Four in 1996 (though UMass' spot later was vacated).

Both coaches knew they had to get on TV. Their scheduling philosophy was literally "anyone, anytime, anywhere." If Kansas wanted to play a three for one, and Chaney had to go to Allen Fieldhouse three times, he would do it. If the opportunity for an ESPN game meant playing at midnight, Calipari would do it. To them nothing was gained by sitting at home playing nobodies in front of nobody. It was risky to an extent, but the strategy proved prescient.

Chaney went to five Elite Eights, and Calipari won the Atlantic 10 five straight times. Temple's rise happened before UMass gained momentum. UMass eventually dethroned Temple, which led to an infamous confrontation following a game in February 1994 at the Mullins Center. Chaney interrupted Calipari's postgame press conference unceremoniously. Things escalated quickly, and the two coaches had to be separated. Chaney even shouted, "I'll kill you."

Knowing Chaney, the anger was very real. But the staging didn't hurt. The rivalry was great for TV, and most UMass-Temple games were on ESPN, even though ESPN didn't air a large Atlantic 10 package.

There also was the earlier sweater rivalry between Thompson and Carnesecca. The fact that—Thompson was 6'10" and Carnesecca was, well, not—made it comical. It also brought millions of eyeballs to television sets. As good as Patrick Ewing (Georgetown) and Chris Mullin (St. John's) were, viewers tuned in just as much to watch the antics of Thompson and Carnesecca. I often think about the likes of Tarkanian, Larry Brown, and Bobby Cremins—guys who flashed across the screen and made you pay attention. I remember University of Houston coach Guy Lewis chewing his towel on the sideline during games. These interesting characters didn't graduate either. The coaches would be there after their stars moved on.

What could have been more compelling than the whole Steve Fisher story? Just before the 1989 NCAA Tournament started, Michigan head coach Bill Frieder made the mistake of telling athletic director Bo Schembechler that he was taking the Arizona State job after the season ended. Schembechler decided that was it for Frieder, and Fisher, his top assistant, would coach the Wolverines in the tournament. Schembechler famously said, "A Michigan man will coach Michigan." Fisher promptly led Michigan to the NCAA championship behind Glen Rice and Rumeal Robinson. A few years later Fisher coached an all-freshman starting five—"The Fab Five"—to the national title game in back-to-back seasons, losing to Duke (1992) and North Carolina (1993). It's hard to surpass Fisher's start. In his first six games as the head coach at Michigan, he went 6–0 and won a national championship. Three years out of five he was in the Final Four and the national title game while Frieder was languishing at Arizona State.

Part of ESPN's success was being savvy with such made-for-TV stories, but a lot of it was grabbing business opportunities. Six months after taking the air for the first time, ESPN was able to show 15 of the 16 opening-round games in the 1980 NCAA Tournament. National networks televised a live game at 11:30 PM (EST) on Thursday and Friday nights, following the local news. ESPN had the rest.

Did ESPN know March Madness would become what it is today, or did it just benefit from the excitement the games generated? It didn't matter one way or the other to tourney-starved fans. The NCAA didn't have other takers for the early rounds, at least not nationally. The market wasn't there. The fascination with the entire tournament had not taken hold beyond the hard-core fans.

Vitale had a huge role in this, too. Remember the Georgetown–Princeton first-round game in 1989, when the Tigers and frumpy coach Pete Carril should have had their UMBC moment? It was the No. 1 vs. No. 16 upset that never happened. Princeton played its slow-down style to perfection and was on the verge of winning before the Hoyas escaped 50–49. Vitale said in the studio that he would hitchhike to Providence, site of the game, if Princeton won.

He should have done it anyway. Regardless, it made for great TV.

I have very fond memories of those early rounds on ESPN. That ended after the 1990 tournament when CBS took exclusive rights to the entire event. ESPN had worked itself out of a job as CBS recognized the enormous value of the early-round games. Of course, the first years CBS aired those rounds on a regional basis, and it caused a huge ruckus. Fortunately, CBS figured that out quickly and added additional partners so that every game could be seen live.

ESPN's success with college hoops had a spin-off effect on other sports. Success in basketball gave the whole network credibility. College basketball and the early coverage of Major League Baseball were high times for the network. Each had long seasons—with weeknight programming—that filled a void on the sports viewing calendar. Think about how well the seasons connect with one another. With baseball ESPN had the Sunday night and Wednesday night games, Monday doubleheaders, and *Baseball Tonight*. Just like college basketball and Bracketology are a natural pairing today, baseball coverage and fantasy baseball were perfect together. The success of basketball led ESPN to other college sports and additional platforms such as ESPN2, ESPNews, and ESPNU (not to mention *ESPN The Magazine*, ESPN Radio, and ESPN.com). Odjakjian believes that there would be no

ESPNU and possibly ESPN2 without college basketball. He's probably right. And the same could be said for the more recent SEC and ACC networks.

All those platforms demanded additional programming, including women's sports. They've become appointment viewing for a lot of people. ESPN originally got the early rounds of the NCAA Tournament because it was willing to broadcast additional sports. Today those sports benefit ESPN because they give the network so much inventory, and the sports benefit because they weren't being covered before ESPN came along. I don't think I knew there was a Women's College World Series before ESPN started showing it. I knew there was this thing in Omaha—the College World Series—but I didn't know anything about it. ESPN changed that, and there was a domino effect across the college sports landscape.

We never used to have Thursday night college football. Now we have college football almost every non-NFL night in the fall. Major conference realignment, though driven by football, had a huge impact on basketball. As a direct result, ESPN now owns the College Football Playoff, the biggest property in the sport. But the conference regular seasons are very significant—even more so than in basketball, and a college football Saturday on the ESPN family of networks is an even bigger deal than a college basketball Saturday (even with its hopefully irreplaceable Bracket Bunker).

The entire model began in the 1980s with the 15 games CBS didn't carry on the first two days of the NCAA Tournament. ESPN doing it and succeeding—whether it's a whole day's worth of games on a weekend or a whole evening's worth on a weeknight—led to a bunch of copycats. ESPN's next level is ESPN+. The addition of Olympic sports at a high quality is great for those fans. One day we may have a Division II or Division III network. All those schools have fans, and their conferences have streaming capabilities.

In my experience ESPN as a company has always valued unique content, including Bracketology. Howie Schwab, who was with ESPN from 1987 through 2013 and was my original editor when Bracketology first appeared on ESPN.com, said, "ESPN has always taken chances. That was something I was proud of in the 26 years I was there. It's something I still think is important to sports fans."

In spite of incredible growth across multiple networks and almost limitless inventory, college basketball and ESPN remain synonymous with one another. CBS has the NCAA Tournament, to be sure, but for just three weeks. The season is now nearly five months long. It starts in early November and runs on ESPN through March with Championship Week and the NIT. The average fan, who sits down on a Tuesday night and wants to watch basketball, is likely putting on one of the ESPN networks. They associate ESPN with college basketball and they associate college basketball with ESPN. We are the paper of record for the sport, if you will. If it doesn't happen on our air at least in the regular season, it's under the radar.

Don't believe me? Look at the recent exploits of Villanova. There was a five-year stretch (2014–18) in which Villanova was far and away the most successful college basketball program in the country. It could be argued that it's one of the greatest stretches in college basketball history. The Wildcats won two national championships. They were a No. 1 seed three times. The other two times they were a No. 2 seed. They *averaged* 33 wins per season. The Wildcats didn't lose back-to-back games once in those five years. In the age of parity and the one-and-done player, it's an incomprehensible feat. Yet, because Villanova plays in a non-ESPN league, its success in the regular season was undervalued. I think if the Wildcats were on ESPN twice a week with those kinds of achievements, there'd be a *30 for 30* documentary about them.

In college basketball there is a power that comes from being on ESPN as opposed to other networks. Even though the inventory is more diversified, the sport and ESPN still go together in a way that benefits every conference that's in partnership with the network. I'm not saying that to shill for the company. It's the reality of how schools and leagues are perceived. What's on our air is considered substantial.

It carries over to the announcers: A person's background doesn't matter as much as the content he or she can produce. Content rules, and I am a direct beneficiary. There is often a preseason gathering of all the people involved in broadcasting each sport at ESPN. Everybody is invited. That means all the commentators, the play-by-play people, the producers, the researchers, etc. If you are involved in that sport, you get an all-expenses-paid trip to Connecticut. One time about 10 or 15 years ago, the speaker for the college basketball gathering was ESPN president George Bodenheimer. I was pretty low on the totem pole at the time, so I was in the back of the room. He started talking about content. He said, "I want you all to think of ESPN as a content company, not a television company."

I hadn't really thought about it that way. Most everyone involved with ESPN wants to get on television. That's just how it is. But think about ESPN Radio, ESPN.com, and all the newer ESPN digital outlets. In a very Disney way, ESPN is a master of repurposing content. An interview with Michael Jordan on the Sunday night *SportsCenter* could live in multiple iterations on multiple platforms within minutes. The content is substantial and it can be repurposed. It doesn't matter if you didn't play, didn't coach, or (in my case) couldn't draw up an inbounds play. If your content is compelling, accurate, and scalable across platforms, it has value.

To its credit ESPN was okay showcasing the short Italian guy with a big nose, who had never taken a class in journalism, broadcasting, or mass communications. Actually, it was one of those experimental platforms, ESPNews, that gave me my start on television. I had been doing the ESPN.com stuff since 1995. Those editors and producers from the early days are the ones who deserve the credit. I didn't understand their business and I surely didn't understand the true value of my content. As it turns out, we were just scratching the surface of what Bracketology could become.

CHAPTER FOUR

More Than
a Hobby

Once ESPN started promoting Bracketology, it took off in popularity. That's good for me, of course, but it also meant that it could no longer be treated as a hobby. It used to be that many fans only cared about college basketball after the Super Bowl, and then the feeling was, *Oh, it's college basketball season. I've seen a couple of games, but I wonder how my team is doing relative to other teams.* Now it's more like, *This year's tournament just ended. What are we going to do now? Let's talk about next year's tournament.*

I suppose it's no different than doing a mock 2021 NFL Draft immediately following the conclusion of the 2020 draft. It speaks to the level of interest and the level of passion that exists for our sport. In my early years, I wasn't doing brackets in April for the next season. But in the last 15 years or so, there has been some form of previewing the following year as soon as the current season ends. When that was first suggested, I remember getting on the phone with editors and saying, "I'm really not comfortable with that. It doesn't have the same statistical rigor. I feel like I'm guessing more than I would want to."

The people in Bristol, Connecticut, said, "But, Joe, it's great content." Eventually they said, "We can add to your compensation." That left me saying, "What a great idea! Why didn't I think of that?"

But it also meant my business model had to change. I attempted to bring some rigor and legitimacy to offseason projections by building algorithms based upon the relative efficiencies of teams from the previous year as well as the percentage of minutes played, which might or might not be returning from that team. Theoretically, an established level of performance exists for returnees. Of course, performances change, and players improve, but some also stabilize or even regress. It's about making a reasonable guesstimate. Say 70 percent of a team's offense is back. What is a reasonable aggregate improvement based on the ages of the returning players? That depends. Is the 30 percent lost because of one 40-minute star, or is it five reserves who played eight minutes per game? You can tweak the weighting and try to make an estimate of how the replacement minutes will be filled. This is a derivative of all the Bill James reading I did in high school and college about the replacement level of baseball players. If you lose a George Brett, you don't get zero production at third base. You get the difference between George Brett and the player who would take his place.

For the 2020–21 college basketball season, somebody—or a combination of somebodies—has to fill Devon Dotson's minutes at Kansas. Now if you're at Kansas, Kentucky, or Duke, you might be replacing the minutes of an NBA first rounder with minutes from a future lottery pick. But if you're a program that is more traditional in how it operates—freshmen become sophomores and upperclassmen, they leave, you recruit, lather, rinse, repeat—that's a different equation. So I build in different levels of replacement minutes based on recruiting ranking, positional needs, and level of conference. Like it or not, a non-Top 100 ACC signee is probably a better player than a non-Top 100 Big West signee. There are some assumptions that can be made to keep projections within reason.

The day after the NCAA Tournament ends, we don't necessarily know who's sticking around. We also don't know the final rankings of the recruiting classes. No one is expecting a 68-for-68 performance more than 11 months in advance. It's not realistic. But we still try for that. During each year's tournament after teams are eliminated, I start building out their profile for the following year. Let's look at an average rotation of seven or eight players. Five are expected back. Another player might be back, but will he first test the waters for the NBA draft? Regardless, as teams are eliminated, I'll have an index of how they're slotting relative to one another for the following season. I always fall behind during the first NCAA weekend because there are more teams being eliminated than I can keep up with. When it gets later in the tournament, there are way fewer teams being eliminated, and I can keep up better.

Not being a recruiting expert, I have to rely on other rankings. I use ESPN's rankings not only because I work for ESPN, but also because I know the guys preparing them, at least enough of them. They are also in the educated guessing business. The rankings create a consistent standard. Until I see an impact freshman on the court, I'll take the experts' word for it. Generally speaking, recruiting gets a lot more emphasis than is immediately warranted. You're almost never signing a player who's going to add 10 wins or even five wins. You're getting a rotation player who's probably not much different from who you're losing. At least that's the way I have to look at it in the offseason. The number of teams that go from 10–20 to 20–10 in one year—even in this day and age with nearly unlimited transfers—is pretty small.

A good contrast would be Big 12 rivals Kansas and Kansas State. In Lawrence, Kansas, we know Bill Self has built a national power. He lost two second-team All-Americans (Dotson and Udoka Azubuike) at the end of the 2019–20 season, but he replaced them with more newcomers of the highest level. We may not know ahead of time which ones are going to rise to be difference-makers, but odds are Kansas is only going to fall so far from its presumptive No. 1 overall seed of 2020. Go farther west in the state to Manhattan, and K-State fans were jacked about a recruiting class ranked as high as No. 18 in the country. I have to be the one to say, "Prove it. You were 11–21 last year and lost the little bit of continuity you had." There is a reason one program is a consistent top seed, and the other is a perennial bubble team.

There was a time when I would run through these exhausting scenarios once after the season ended (sometimes even the day after). I might then update them once after the draft—when we knew who was really going and who wasn't—and a final time around the start of practice in October. Now there's so much player movement. It's a constantly changing landscape. There is way more variance. Every morning after the season until spring semesters end in May (in a normal year), I look up the latest transfers and try to determine the level of impact on their teams and those around them. Then I adjust our look-ahead bracket accordingly.

Right after we released one of my early brackets for the 2020–21 season this past spring, Arizona State signed a top 10 player. ASU fans wanted a new bracket the next day to see the impact. With our algorithm if a school adds a true 30- to 35-minute star, it might be enough to move from the bubble to, say, an 8 or 9 seed. Conversely, if a key contributor unexpectedly declares for the draft or transfers out, his former team might go from a No. 10 seed to First Four Out. That would be a lot of movement, but it can and does happen. It won't be long before the demand for updated brackets at certain periods of the offseason is as great as the peak time of February and early March. The desire for new information and the technology to produce it has changed everything, as is the case in so many endeavors. Nobody in college basketball was thinking this way 20 or 25 years ago. I could fold up my laptop after Selection Sunday and head to the golf course and not worry too much about the frequency of offseason Bracketology or the level of accuracy required.

Here's another unintended consequence of offseason Bracketology. There are schools looking at these updates and using them for scheduling purposes. They might call and ask, "We can get a home-and-home with so-and-so. How good do you think they're going to be?" Some teams are looking to beef up their schedules, and others, obviously, are not. That leads to a different kind of call. "We were just offered a chance to play State U, and our coach thinks they might be too good. What do you think?"

These conversations have taken place forever. The difference is there is now a more quantifiable way to go about making such scheduling decisions. It's another example of how Bracketology has become a year-round enterprise, at least from a data standpoint. Literally every morning I look at the transactions in college basketball from all available sources and aggregate the headlines accordingly. Most of those headlines are only tweaking a team in invisible ways. But three invisible tweaks for a team might add up to a visible adjustment. If I don't keep up with it in the offseason, it would be like letting a month go by during the season without entering all the results. I would be monumentally behind. The only difference in the offseason is that I'm not waiting for West Coast games to end. I'm doing it over coffee the next morning.

In the last few years, particularly as I have transitioned my own life to be primarily self-employed, I've put myself out there and made myself more available to provide information on scheduling, program building, and marketing. This could take the shape of a formal consulting arrangement with a school. More often it's just a quick piece of advice. "Hey, a buddy of mine is an assistant coach at such-and-such school. What do you think of them adding Team X?" As big as the sport is, it's still a pretty tight community of people who work in college basketball. And the word gets out. My only requirement is that any "offseason" work ends when a new season begins. The evaluation of all teams must be neutral, or there is no credibility in the results. I stand by the mantra: "Check your biases at the door."

If this sounds like committee-speak, that's because it is. Something I'm really proud of is the shared vocabulary of all things Bracketology, including the committee's statements. You see and hear it with their in-season conference calls, February's reveal of the top 16 teams, and, of course, the Selection Sunday interviews. Just as I would, they say, "We rated this team based on X, Y, and Z." It's almost as if we could finish each other's sentences.

I know that probably sounds arrogant and unintention-ally big-headed. But when the committee chair went on TV two decades ago (if he went on TV at all) he or she wasn't talking much about quality wins, breakdown of schedules, recent performance, or team efficiency. You can be sure that he or she is today. All of these things are the result of the public being educated about what goes on in that room.

Everyone wants to be the best at what they do, and some years I can make that claim better than others. But the single greatest contribution of Bracketology to college basketball has been the education of the masses on what the selection and seeding process really entails. It was a completely closed system. Also credit Greg Shaheen for realizing that every-body would benefit if they opened it up a little. It's been a totally positive evolution. For instance, coaches who used to have to guess on putting their schedules together no longer have to do so. That has created the opportunity for me and many others to be involved in scheduling. We all have an overlapping skillset and a uniqueness to our expertise that can be valuable.

Another thing I never would have anticipated is assisting ESPN's college basketball programming team. I start sending them rankings as early as possible so they can be used as a resource for the upcoming season's television schedule. It doesn't take a bracketologist to put the Kansas vs. Baylor game on "Big Monday." But figuring out the tonnage of additional inventory takes months. When, for example, the network fills the slot for a late Tuesday matchup on ESPNU, it might be the seventh best game that night. But programming has to figure out how to get the seventh best game instead of the 77th best. And they have to do it months in advance.

Even though ESPN no longer produces the Bracket Busters concept, it absolutely produces games that bust the eventual bracket. Specifically, the ESPN networks are airing countless games involving likely bubble teams. Not surprisingly, these games are also good for ratings. After all, ESPN is still in the "eyeball business."

As am I. Which is why the content I'm producing for broadcast is more immediate and perhaps less analytical than my work for ESPN.com. Think of it as real-time exit polling as opposed to waiting until the election is over. If a producer at the SEC Network, which ESPN owns, has Alabama vs. Georgia in late February, that game might not get a sentence on ESPN.com. But its viewers from the SEC will want to know every possible outcome scenario as the game unfolds.

Of course, we're still going to see Kentucky on our air 20 times. If Kentucky was playing an intramural team—or maybe even *fielding* an intramural team—we're going to show the game because it's Kentucky. Similarly, we're going to get Duke, Kansas, and Gonzaga: all the big names that are in the leagues where ESPN is the primary outlet. ESPN knows what moves the needle at the top of the scale. I'm putting my finger in the middle. I'm not advising them on Kansas; I'm advising them on Kansas State. I'm not advising them on Duke; I'm advising them on Wake Forest. Did we miss the boat on San Diego State in 2019–20? Absolutely. But the goal of the offseason in terms of working with the programming folks is to miss as few boats as possible.

The concept of an offseason is disappearing before my eyes, but there still is one—at least compared to the time between the Super Bowl and Selection Sunday. The easiest way to describe that period is to say I'm a "walking, talking, ranking machine." For six weeks I live in a spreadsheet that doubles as a dynamic seed list. Every result that impacts one of the teams on that sheet—and by Super Bowl Sunday, there are about 100 listed, including all potential at-large selections and the top teams in all the typical one-bid leagues—impacts the rest of the seed list in real time.

Occasionally, there are results from the previous night that I haven't factored in. Maybe I missed a game or fell asleep because of a really late ending—Saint Mary's at Pacific in four overtimes, anyone? More likely is that I already sent win/lose scenarios to the overnight *SportsCenter* and don't need to hang for the last final. Yes, that's cheating, but a tired bracketologist is a less accurate bracketologist!

In the morning I'll recalculate my own metrics and cross-check the daily NCAA Evaluation Tool (NET) and other third-party numbers, in particular KenPom and ESPN's Strength of Record (SOR). Eventually I'll get to all six rankings that are included by the NCAA on its team sheets, as well as the latest quad breakdowns for every team. As the NET rankings change, a Quad One win on Tuesday might not be Quad One on Wednesday. I might need to know that for broadcast or other content purposes. The bottom line is to make sure I have each day's information as if that day was Selection Sunday. My master spreadsheet is essentially a distillation of every relevant team sheet in a single document and for my eyes only. Although updates can be made throughout the day, the overnight baseline best approximates what committee members would be seeing. It might take an hour or two during the week, depending on the number of games the night before, or a Sunday update could take four to six hours following a full slate of 150-plus Saturday games.

Once I'm done with the data, I scrub the team order as needed to re-rank a full 1–68 seed list. The top seeds could change, or more likely the dreaded Last Four In/ First Four Out groupings will change. I also have to check the conference leaders in every league for AQ (automatic qualifier) purposes. Let's say Belmont passes Murray State at the top of the OVC. That result would put the Bruins in our projected field and drop the Racers into the at-large pool. Or if a new Ivy League leader is a No. 12 seed when its predecessor was a No. 14, all teams from all conferences in that seed range could move.

We repeat this entire process daily with increasing scrutiny from early November through Selection Sunday morning. Whether one game or 150 games were played the night before, there is a new seed list every day. I don't always update the actual bracket, but the data is in place for when those daily—and sometimes hourly—updates are requested later in the season. I also give a passing glance each Monday when the new polls come out. Even though these media and coaches rankings aren't part of the formal process, we know anecdotally that a consensus No. 1 team in the polls—even if it has a much poorer NET ranking—is still likely to be a No. 1 seed. That's just the way it is, and it's my job to keep track of anything that might formally or informally influence the process. That's the data and rankings part of what I do.

The walking, talking part is what separates me from most other bracketologists. Every Friday after the major conference seasons begin, I send a weekend preview across the network based on the upcoming schedule. That update goes to every production truck and studio show, driving many storylines of our coverage. Although not the case all season long, nor should it be, by February we'll be talking about the postseason prospects of pretty much every game on our air. You can't ignore it. It's the storyline every fan is tracking for their team.

What I'm doing is quantifying and framing the content. When the pregame comes on before, say, North Carolina State at Clemson, the talent might say, "Clemson is looking to end a four-game losing streak and stay on the right side of the bubble, and N.C. State is hoping to solidify a good seed in the tournament." Before I became a walking, talking bracket machine, we would have to speculate. It wasn't as scientific.

If a key "bubble game" is on a weeknight, I've probably already sent a mid-afternoon update. If not—because of another commitment, a travel snafu, or the dog swallowing my homework—I'll often hear from talent, a producer in the truck, a graphics person, or the studio host or analyst who is doing halftime and wants to frame the game as accurately as we can.

From the network's point of view, it helps if everyone is singing from the same hymnal. And I don't take it lightly that I've been entrusted to sometimes write that hymn or at least the words to the hymn. There's no way to do it half-speed. I'll do a midweek bracket and seed list in January with the same rigor as Selection Saturday night, following every step just as the committee would.

The only way I get through it relatively quickly each day is—unlike the actual committee—I don't have to get nine other people to agree with me. I'm a committee of one. I'm unilateral. And, boy, wouldn't that be a great way to live?

There are other ways my life is different on December 1 than March 1. On December 1 I'm doing the data and the seed list, but I'm not feeding the broadcast side of things. If I want to do two or three days' worth of data during the November tournaments, I can. If I don't want to enter the Thanksgiving games because I'm in a food coma, I can wait until Saturday or Sunday.

I usually don't let things slide, though, if only because you have to be more than a little nerdy to do this kind

of work. I'm also a reasonably driven person who understands the pressure to produce content is much different in
November than it is in February. We'll do an ESPN.com
bracket every week in November and December, but we do
one every day in late February and early March.

Someday we may get to daily brackets for the entire
season, but we're not there yet. But there are times earlier in
the year when I might be supplying content for ESPN tournaments in Orlando, Florida; Anaheim, California; Nassau,
Bahamas; or Lahaina, Hawaii. If there are legitimate bubble
teams in those tournaments, I might produce a mini-update,
mentioning, "These are games we might end up talking about
in March."

Intuitively, fans know that if I say their team is Last
Four In on December 1, there's way more variability than
if I say Last Four In on March 1. If I say you're Last Four
In, chances are incredibly high you're no more than one
seed better or one seed worse than that. In other words, if
I say your team is Last Four In, it's not going to be a No. 3
seed when the actual bracket is revealed. You'd better not
stub your toe the rest of the way. We can't make that claim
in December, but the games are still just as meaningful. In
something like the ACC/Big Ten Challenge, a matchup
between Penn State and Georgia Tech could be critical.
It may not get an audience like North Carolina against

Michigan State, but in my world it's more impactful. I'll likely be watching the potential bubble games more closely even if they're on ESPNU at 9:30 PM instead of ESPN at 8:00 PM. That's okay. They're all good games, and I'm happy to live in my world. And just because I may not be going on the air in November or December to talk about it, chances are the results will come up in February and March.

Before Christmas I can do my numbers by noon and then be done for the day until the games start that night. I'm not taping segments. I'm not writing columns. I'm not doing many interviews on radio stations in local markets. I'm not giving interviews to print reporters. I'm definitely not setting up live shots for halftime. The best days include a St. Joe's assignment or a local game involving another Philly team. It's just a whole different level of demand for my time. By February the data is getting better, and my observations are getting better. I've seen more games. I've seen more teams. I'm reading more. I'm tracking more stats. Like in the NFL, if you're scouting the Green Bay Packers, you probably know a lot more in Week 14 than you do in Week Two.

* * *

I've been asked many times, "Where is the Bracket Bunker and what does it look like?" There are actually three different bunkers. The real bunker is in Bristol, Connecticut, at ESPN headquarters. It's an infrequently used studio in the basement of one of the older buildings. It's got that backdrop behind me with all the cutouts of players, mascots, and logos. It's also got Last Four In and First Four Out charts, which we update in real time. It's basically yours truly, a desk, and a robo-camera that feeds into what's called the "wraps" control room, which is short for wrap-ups. When a live game throws it to the studio at halftime or between games—let's say on "Big Monday" with Kevin Negandhi, Seth Greenberg, and LaPhonso Ellis—I'm working with that production group. I'm in the bunker, and they can cut to me anytime, but I'm not in the same studio. I'm not even in the same building. I'm where I can work on my own with a half-dozen games on.

They also have multiple monitors on the main college basketball set. Greenberg and Phonz, Sean Farnham and Dalen Cuff, or whoever makes up the analyst pair that night, are watching for different things than I am. If they're coming on at halftime of Indiana vs. Michigan State, they have to be watching that game closely to say, "Cassius Winston really doesn't have it tonight." Meanwhile, I might be watching San Diego State vs. Utah State. When they cut to me, I'll be ready to say, "We could lose a No. 1 seed tonight. San Diego State is down with four minutes to go."

To this day, I'm still amazed at how it all comes together so seamlessly. That's because the really smart guys are the ones off camera. Barry Sacks and Billy Graff originated and perfected the bunker. Rob Lemley, Chris Riviezzo, Steve Oling, Jerry Daniels, and so many others are the producers and directors who make me look good. The bunker is isolated for both the aesthetics and the schtick. It's like I'm the mad scientist in his laboratory, shaking up the test tubes and seeing what bubbles out. Bill Walton likes to say I'm in a cave, basically doing my own thing. And he's not wrong. But it's also wonderful because I can keep track of all the games I need to at any given time.

The broadcast schedule might start at 7:00 PM, but we all meet at 5:00 or 6:00. I could say, "Here are some things that might happen tonight based on the schedule." I include the games that are on our air as well as games I'll be tracking elsewhere. The response can be anything from "Let's put Joe on at halftime of the main ESPN game," or "The SEC Network game in Tuscaloosa wants Joe at the under-8:00 timeout of the first half." Many times we're reiterating information that was shared earlier in the day in my network update, but we're in a visual medium. It's usually better to have the person who created the information saying it as opposed to just listing it on the screen.

All of this is easiest when I'm in Connecticut, which is why ESPN prefers me there. They can set me up in the bunker with one camera and one microphone and can beam me into any broadcast on an ESPN platform. Sometimes those decisions are made on the fly. A remote producer may call the control room from Tucson, Arizona, because a game is unfolding unexpectedly and ask, "Can we have Joe talk about what it means if this upset holds?"

That's kind of cool. Actually, it's not kind of cool; it's incredibly cool. And that's what makes my slice of the Bracketology pie different from most everyone else's. I'm the on-call pundit for the network that has the most college basketball games. The key word is "games." Understanding that I do nothing of global importance is, well, important. There are a lot of people who have real jobs out there, and I'm not one of them. But I'm also mindful of the fact that in this segment of the sports world, like it or not, I am a trusted authority. I try to take that very seriously while not taking myself too seriously. I'm the messenger more than the message. It's supposed to be at least a little bit fun. We're not reporting the latest economic crisis or health scare. We're doing a daily seed list.

When you see me in a nice suit and it's well lit and there are graphics and a nice set behind me, that's in Connecticut. When you see the fake backdrop that says, "ESPN College Basketball" and nothing else, that's in Bunker No. 2: my basement. We've added lighting and enhanced sound and a better camera setup, but it's still basically an iPad with a souped-up app to transmit broadband video. There are now all kinds of in-home setups across the industry. It's not just sports. We saw anchors doing news hits from their homes during the worst of the coronavirus. We'll further enhance my home setup, too. We've talked about putting a live monitor behind me for real-time graphics like "Last Four In" and "First Four Out." Then I could turn around and talk about it like a weatherman. We're just not that far along yet.

There's also one other bunker. At the really peak times of the season during Championship Week, I'm not always able to be in Connecticut. If I'm at the Atlantic 10 Tournament with St. Joe's or on some other assignment, Bunker No. 3 would be wherever I can set up a camera. I may have to take lamp shades off in a hotel room, point desk lamps at my head, and fire up an iPhone propped up against the minibar to get on TV in front of bad curtains and ugly paintings. Just as Air Force One is whatever plane the president is on, I guess the bunker is whatever studio, basement, or hotel room I'm in.

* * *

The impact of Bracketology far exceeds just predicting teams for a basketball tournament. Other brackets have occurred since Bracketology took off. In 2016 there were brackets of Republican presidential nominees—who knew that Donald Trump was going to be the 12-seed who beat the 5? ESPN televises the MLB Home Run Derby and puts the players in a bracket. But my personal favorite was "barketology."

Early in 2016 Purina partnered with the Westminster Kennel Club (WKC). The company was looking to do a promotion around the Westminster Dog Show at Madison Square Garden. There are seven breed categories, and a winner is chosen in each. The winners then compete to be "Best in Show." In other words WKC has its own Elite Eight. Purina created an online bracket contest and offered a million-dollar prize for a perfect bracket. The winner also got a one-year supply of Purina dog food. And that's not just any Purina dog food. It's Purina Pro Plan, which I learned was the nutrition of choice of nine of the last 11 Best in Show winners. I was asked to be the voice of this contest.

I got on a call in early January for the February roll-out with the Purina people, people from Westminster, the ad agency that was running the promotion, and a website builder. There was going to be an introductory video, and I was supposed to memorize 128 breeds and be able to speak about all of them—from the Maltese Mountain Husky to the Pomeranian Shih Tzu. It was detailed, to say the least.

I finally said, "Gang, I've got to tell you, I'm the paid talent here so I'll do whatever you tell me, but this is really dull."

Finally, it was my wife, Pam, who nailed it. She said, "You should call it 'barketology.'"

The creative people all thought that was great. The Westminster folks, who are really serious dog people, were aghast. Eventually I said to the Purina people, "Isn't the goal here to sell more dog food? Then we need to appeal to the masses, not just to the insiders. The insiders already know about your dog food. We need to go after basic dog owners with something fun." So that was how barketology was born. We soon completed a barketology video with a bunch of dog and bracket puns. It was so bad it was good.

A month later I went to New York City and yucked it up on a media tour. There's a building in Manhattan that houses a bunch of the Sirius XM radio stations. I did drop-ins on a host of sports and entertainment stations to promote the contest. It turns out actor Ryan Reynolds was doing a media tour that same day for his new movie *Deadpool*. Being a locked-in bracketologist in season, I didn't know who Ryan Reynolds was. In the green room at Sirius, there were two congregations. There was my little posse and Reynolds and his really big posse. Visiting the restroom at one point, there was Reynolds. As we were coming out, he said, "You're that bracket guy." I said, "Oh, yeah, I'm Joe Lunardi. What's your name?" To his credit, Reynolds ignored my ignorance, and we went about our business.

Well, my wife and daughters freaked out when they heard of my *faux pas*. How was I supposed to know who Ryan Reynolds was? Needless to say, I do now. More importantly, barketology was a commercial and creative success. About 350,000 people filled out a dog bracket. And I learned a few things along the way. It was all good.

After all, it's really wild to have invented something so popular, even accidentally. Look at the way people filled their free time during the shutdown caused by the coronavirus. There were brackets all over the place. There was a bracket of James Bond movies, *SportsCenter* hosts, and breakfast cereals, just to name a few. ESPN.com writer Bradford Doolittle did a segment called the "Second-Chance World Series." Each MLB franchise had its best representative, a team that went to the World Series but didn't win it all. I was captivated by that as were a lot of people. Even a fictitious bracket drew its share of attention. Doolittle created the rules and selected the teams. But it was based on common bracket philosophy, pairing teams that may have had less talent with others that on paper should win every time.

Obviously there were brackets long before I came along. The field of 64 existed before the word Bracketology. But I do feel the concept has been elevated a lot in recent years.

Full disclosure: I wasn't even the first person to predict the bracket for the NCAA Tournament. Steve Wieberg, a college columnist for *USA TODAY*, did it several years before I did. He was, to his credit, very accurate, especially considering how little information was available publicly back then. But Bracketology didn't really take off until ESPN grabbed it probably because clever editors at ESPN.com— guys like Ron Buck, Andy Glockner, Brett Edgerton, Nick Pietruszkiewicz, and Tony Moss—and later ESPN productions knew exactly how to leverage it.

That audience—the serious college basketball fan—is the one for whom the bracket has the most meaning. The average reader of *USA TODAY* isn't necessarily opening the paper to find a projected bracket. But a reader or viewer of ESPN's college basketball platforms in January, February, and March is looking for a bracket seven days a week and twice on Sunday!

It might surprise you that someone who makes his living predicting college basketball tournament brackets would think there is too much emphasis placed on how teams perform in that tournament. But it's true. I believe that there is a disproportionate emphasis on how a team performs in March versus how it performed all season. It's often how coaches, programs, and conferences are evaluated. It's not unlike college football where there is probably a disproportionate emphasis on bowl games. Any statistician or really any reasonable person will tell you that four months' worth of data—or in the case of college basketball, four months' worth of results—is more valuable and more telling than four weeks' worth. Coaches, players, programs, and leagues still get evaluated by March, no matter how much we say that's the wrong way to do it. Bracketology absolutely feeds into that mind-set.

Maybe I'm hypocritical to promote it, but I didn't invent the system. I'm just playing the hand that's been dealt. Bill Self can go 33–3 and lose to Northern Iowa in the second round of the NCAA Tournament and be considered a failure. That doesn't make it right, but the emphasis on the tournament and the postseason was here long before Bracketology came along. But I've probably made it worse. If Kansas had ended up a No. 1 seed in the 2020 tournament, as everyone expected, it would have been their ninth No. 1 seed in Self's 17 years there. KU never has been worse than a No. 4 seed under Self. For 17 straight years, they've been seeded to be a Sweet 16 team. Have they been to 17 straight Sweet 16s? Of course not; no one has.

But as a fan, wouldn't you like to start every season thinking, *We're going to end up being one of the best 16 teams in the country? Chances are we'll be playing in the second weekend of the tournament.* Of course you would take that. You're not going to the Final Four every time you're a No. 1 seed. It just means you have a better chance than every other team in the country except the other three top seeds. I would love to be a fan of a program that had a chance to blow nine No. 1 seeds in 17 years. You're going to go to your share of Final Fours and play in your share of national championship games. That's playing the probabilities. They reality is that since the bracket fully expanded in 1985 there has been only one tournament in which all four No. 1 seeds made it to the Final Four. Even more ironic is that same year (2008) marks the only national title for Self at Kansas.

Smart athletic directors and administrators can, should, and hopefully do look at the bigger picture. A coach should get a contract extension for nine No. 1 seeds—not fired for not winning a corresponding number of championships. I believe it's actually harder to earn a No. 1 seed than to reach a Final Four because a top seed represents a season's worth of excellent basketball whereas reaching the sport's final weekend represents only four games.

My colleague at ESPN, Seth Greenberg, says that even being on the bubble means you're having a great season because that means you're among the top sixth of all teams in the country. I would argue it's even better than that. After the automatic qualifiers, there are 36 at-large bids. With 357 Division I schools as of the 2020–21 season, an at-large team is actually one of the top 10 percent of teams that season. Beyond the perennial participants, the NCAA Tournament bubble is a great aspirational point. When I'm approached by schools in the offseason, I'll respond by saying, "What can you do to get in the bubble conversation?" Because a lot of them are saying, "Joe, we don't want to be in your First Four Out." And I'll say, "Sure you do, especially if you haven't been in the tournament in a while." Being in First Four Out means you're one bounce of a ball from being in the Last Four In or better. So go for it. Just like if you're a No. 1 seed nine times, you can't help but get a championship or two. If you're on the bubble nine times, you're going to earn your share of bids, and that's fine.

Being in the center of Bracketology has its perks. Toward the end of the 2019–20 season, I was approached about producing a Joe Lunardi bobblehead. How cool is that? I did think the bobblehead would be a bit taller, but it turned out true to life—big head, small body. Maybe it's more accurate than I want to admit.

For the bulk of the years I've been doing Bracketology, I had a real job as the head of marketing and communications at Saint Joseph's University in Philadelphia. It was an important job for me. And I took it and the people, who worked with me, very seriously. I wouldn't change it or take anything back. But in the back of my mind, it always lingered: what could happen if I devoted the bulk of my professional energy, at least during the season, to Bracketology? If I no longer had a full-time job and could run with this permanently, what would happen? Would I get on TV more? Check. Would I get my own show? Check. Would somebody help me write a book about Bracketology? Check. Could I have some endorsements? Check. Are there speaking engagements to be had? Check.

I don't think I ever thought about a bobblehead, though, so it pays to be open to possibilities. For the first time, I'm not passively pursuing them. I'm suggesting ideas as opposed to waiting by the phone to hear others' suggestions. Mostly, it's just fun. I tell myself that every day during the season. If I'm up late or get cranky, I think, *You know, Joe, you could still have a real job. I'm getting paid to track basketball results and talk about what they mean.* Most sports fans would say, "Sign me up for that." And I am mindful of that every day. If I ever get jaded or sound entitled, that's when somebody needs to talk some sense into me. If that was ever the case, I should either get out of this, gracefully pass it on to someone else, or get another job. I would like to ride this wave for a few more years. I'm young enough and healthy enough to be a little kid again and take this professional hobby to another level. Who among us wouldn't want to do that?

People told me for years that I should write a book or have my own merchandise. I always pooh-poohed it. Maybe it was false humility, but I just didn't think there was enough interest beyond the obvious peak times of the calendar. It was a series of events that convinced me otherwise. For example, I was at a minor league baseball game a couple of years ago in Montgomery, Alabama. It was a fun night with my nephew and his wife. I was sitting at the game, eating my helmet sundae, when the general manager came over with the in-house video people and put me on the video board. A bracketologist had never come to watch the Montgomery Biscuits.

Later, with this book project already underway, all doubt disappeared in the wake of the cancellation of the 2020 NCAA Tournament. Like every other college basketball fan, I was incredibly sad when the news came out. I might have been even sadder this year than others because it was such a great season with so many storylines. There are always storylines, but three of the top five teams in the 2020 tournament were going to be from outside the power conferences. The national player of the year (Obi Toppin of Dayton) was from outside the Power Five. It seems to me that the level of interest in the 2020 tourney was going to be off the charts. We were all excited to see how it was going to play out.

We were all focused on the bracket that wasn't. As society shut down, sports fans were looking for activities, and the

NCAA Tournament was at the top of everyone's mind. It probably got a disproportionate amount of attention because of the timing. Had the pandemic begun in the middle of August, we would not have been talking as much about brackets.

I got home that Friday of Championship Week and then sat around and moped for a couple of days. At around 6:00 PM on Sunday night, it only seemed logical to post what the bracket would have looked like had the tournament been held. It wasn't much of a leap from there to see how the tournament would have played out. Even though I'm just a little bit better than average when it comes to picking who's going to win once the field is set, that didn't stop me from trying.

A lot of people had computer simulations going, but I decided to play it out differently. We were all grieving the loss of something important to us. I'm not equating it to real-life loss, of course, but it was a loss. At 6:40 PM on the following Tuesday, the first game would have tipped off at the First Four in Dayton. At noon on Thursday, the full tournament would have started. I decided to create the drama of the results, the upsets, the advancing in the brackets—basically the fun of the NCAA Tournament in our own small way. With more than 240,000 Twitter followers, I decided that was the best platform.

I wasn't the only one who had the idea, but for a change, I wasn't interested in statistical rigor. There are people with bigger hard drives who knew how to do that. No one else brought my history of how a tournament typically unfolds in terms of proportionality of upsets, the number of Cinderellas, the major conferences advancing, and all of that. I wanted to find the UMBCs and the George Masons and make it realistic. If you run a simulation 10,000 times, the No. 1 seeds are all going to advance. In real life No. 16 seed UMBC actually won one time (in 2018). No. 1 seeds get upset, though very rarely in the first round. I tried to play it out that way.

At noon on Thursday, my tournament started. I acted like a reporter, advancing the game and then posted a running story at halftime. At the end of the game, I'd recap the outcome with a lead paragraph of about 240 characters. I filed the game story about two hours after it would have started. I repeated this through each game, each round, following the typical timeline of events. When I started this exercise, I didn't know who was going to win. I literally went game by game. I'd get to Thursday night and notice that one region had too much chalk, or all the teams from one conference were winning and adjust accordingly.

But there was no mathematical component. I looked at each game as a potential matchup and decided who I thought would win and by what score. In the back of my mind, just like if you were filling out your own bracket—for amusement only—you would get to the end and say, "I have all the No. 1 seeds advancing. That would never happen." So I tried to circumvent that ahead of time.

When I got to the second and third rounds, I thought, *It's time for one of the No. 1 seeds to lose.* Which game looks the most plausible for an upset? Call it a bracket of plausibility. I had a little bit of fun, too. I had Duke and Kentucky play in the Sweet 16 in the Midwest Region. I pulled out the play-by-play sheet of the Christian Laettner game in Philadelphia in 1992 and then reversed it. It was Kentucky who hit the miracle shot to win in overtime 104–103. As I was teasing that one—by the Sweet 16 there were more frequent in-game updates—people started to notice that I was following the 1992 script. In the next round, Kentucky played Wisconsin, who gave the Wildcats a heartbreaking loss in the 2015 Final Four when they were 38–0. So I reversed that game as well. Kentucky became champions of the "revenge region."

I've been friendly with Baylor coach Scott Drew for a long time. Many years ago, he was probably the first big-time coach to call me to find out where his then-bubble team stood. But in the Twitter tourney, Baylor lost to St. Mary's in the second round, making the Bears the first No. 1 seed to go down. St. Mary's had dropped a game earlier in the season in four overtimes on a missed goaltending call. The conference later admitted that the call was missed, but it couldn't change the result. I had St. Mary's pull this upset in the fourth overtime on a goaltended basket just because it was fun. For the most part, everything in my bracket was genuinely plausible.

I was stunned that people got upset with some of my results. Nobody loves mid-majors more than I do, but in the first round, I had Belmont getting blown out by Duke in Greensboro, North Carolina. The Belmont coach immediately tweeted his disagreement. The Belmont sports information folks then tweeted the whole history of every time Belmont had played Duke, including in the tournament, telling how close it was. They wondered why I wouldn't fashion a similar result. Well, this was a No. 14 seed playing a No. 3 seed in their own backyard. Duke also likes to run it up, and the Blue Devils probably would have gotten their ears chewed about their past close calls against Belmont. The fact that I made it a blowout was clearly within the range of plausibility, but it made one fanbase unhappy. My response was to remind everyone that even in a simulated tournament, there are 67 losers and one winner. Plus, *it was just a Twitter tournament!*

For everyone who wrote and called it a dumb exercise, there were plenty of others who bought in. Literally, the

Monday morning after what would have been the first week-end, I woke up to messages on my phone: "I'm in withdrawal from Lunardi's tournament. When will it resume?"

It resumed on Thursday evening just like the real tour-nament would have. There were millions of engagements on social media. We were all longing for college basketball. And I'm not ashamed to admit that I probably did it as much for me as for the public. That's the impact of Bracketology. My more-than-a-hobby profession even drew eyeballs when the real NCAA Tournament was cancelled because people still looked my way to get their fix of college basketball. That's pretty neat.

CHAPTER FIVE

The Not-So-Secret Formula

I'm asked all the time about my formula for determining teams that will be selected to the NCAA Tournament. The most honest answer? There isn't one. Beauty is in the eye of the beholder.

So how do bracketologists know what the Selection Committee's preferences might be in a particular year? The snarky answer is we don't. There are simply the personal preferences of 10 individual committee members. Pick any endeavor. Take 10 people off the street, ask them the same question, and you might get 10 different answers. And you might get 10 newer answers on Tuesday to the very same question you asked on Monday. That's life.

Every committee member is entitled to, and in fact expected to, vote according to his or her conscience, weighing whatever data points and observations they see fit. Any formula or emphasis implemented by Joe Lunardi, Jerry Palm, or, for that matter, James Naismith, could be vastly different from that year's committee chair or any of its members. My great old Aunt Henrietta said it all the time, "Guiseppe, some people like chocolate, and some like vanilla. Who knows why?" We can apply that thinking to the NCAA selection and seeding process.

Some committee members mostly watch games. They're not looking at any metrics. Others are heavily into the numbers and don't care as much about what happens on TV or their personal observation. The truth (as usual) is somewhere in the middle. I'm often amused by the advocacy—and criticism—of the so-called "basketball people" in the room. These committee members are presumably making basketball judgments based upon what they see, commonly referred to as the "eye test."

I've probably created the opposite impression: that I'm a numbers nerd with my own work. No one who thinks that has ever seen my checkbook register, which would fail any eye test. So although it may be true that I personally prefer metrics-based methods, Bracketology has to take on more of a hybrid approach. I watch a lot of games. And I track almost every game, at least those among the top 100 or so teams. That means I'm tracking as many games as possible as they're going on. I look at box scores and summaries after the fact. Sometimes I look at play-by-play sheets beyond the box scores to see the trends of a game. If it's a key matchup in February between two bubble teams, I want to know if somebody blew a 20-point lead, if somebody had a great comeback, or if a key guy played only eight minutes because of foul trouble.

All of this work helps me form a judgment to mimic the committee's monitoring system. Their process takes every piece of relevant information into account. There are 10 members of the committee. There are 32 Division I conferences. Each committee member has primary and secondary monitoring assignments as they crisscross the country throughout a season. A member based in Kansas City might have the Big 12 as a primary assignment and the Southland or Conference USA as a secondary assignment. At any point in the process, he or she could be called upon by fellow members to provide information about a team or teams from those conferences. A member might say to the Big 12 monitor, "TCU upset Baylor, but I don't know anything about the game." The monitor might say, "Baylor's top player picked up two fouls in four minutes and didn't play the rest of the first half. They fell behind by 15 on the road and couldn't come all the way back."

Similar information is communicated periodically throughout the season. Monitors have regular calls with the league offices where conference staff—maybe an associate commissioner for men's basketball and the conference public relations person—report on injuries, suspensions, player absences, illnesses, or quirks in games, like a team that normally shoots 40 percent on three-pointers going 2-for-19 to sway an outcome.

In the 2019–20 season, St. Mary's lost a West Coast Conference game by a point in four overtimes against Pacific when a clear goaltending call wasn't made. The play wasn't administered incorrectly; it just wasn't correctable by rule. It was a judgment call that in retrospect was plainly missed. But St. Mary's, a potential bubble team, dropped a game that could be considered a bad loss down the road. I'm sure this information was communicated by the WCC office to its committee monitors. It could have come to pass in March that St. Mary's was firmly on the bubble. A committee member might have brought up the January loss at Pacific. That's when the conference monitor could say, "The Gaels were victimized by a blown call."

We know these conversations take place. We just don't know how it translates into the committee's secret balloting process. Ultimately, it is the existence of that balloting that makes identifying a specific reason for any vote impossible. The base information for committee members lives on what are called team sheets, which are now public. We can go to the NCAA website and look at exactly the same data and in the same format that the committee sees. This didn't used to be the case.

Whether it's for an at-large spot or for a particular seed, let's say we're in the room looking at St. Bonaventure and Georgia. Both could already be in the field based on prior votes, and the committee would be debating who's a No. 6 seed and who's a No. 7 seed. Someone will ask to compare them head to head. So the NCAA staff will display the two team sheets side by side. The most visible information on the team sheets is the sorting of that team's season by quads (i.e. Quad One, Quad Two, Quad Three, and Quad Four, depending upon the difficulty of the game). The quads are derived on a sliding scale based on the site of the game. For instance, a home game is considered Quad One if the opponent is ranked 1–30 by the NCAA Evaluation Tool (NET). A road game slots into Quad One if the opponent is ranked 1–75.

All of a team's results are displayed by quadrants, including date, site, score, and whether or not it was a conference game. The latter gives some insight into whether the team intentionally scheduled the game to perhaps boost (or weaken) its postseason profile. Ultimately, each committee member is starting with a team's NET ranking and then moving through its quads. Viewing each team's results in the context of who they played is an essential baseline. Beyond that, every committee member is free to assign any level of importance to any piece of information available. Their method can be anything from "I'm going to make my picks based strictly on AP rankings" to "I'm not going to look at the team sheet at all. I don't care what it says. I saw that team 12 times, and it was terrible."

This is the beloved human element. At the end of the day, we're looking at 10 individual formulas if there are any formulas at all. But there are past practices. Otherwise Bracketology has no basis. We have to be able to reverse engineer the past in order to predict future results.

Consider these facts about the committee: its members serve five-year terms. Barring the cycle getting off-kilter—a member could change jobs and no longer be eligible—generally there are two new members every year. The entire committee thus recycles every five years.

Part of my work is to anticipate and adjust for these changes in membership and how that might translate to different voting patterns. We're not talking bias but degrees of emphasis. One committee might collectively value strength of schedule; another could get stuck on quality wins.

Although it sometimes seems the committee does one thing one year and something totally different the next, we must remember every season is itself different. And these are not 10 random people off the street. These are 10 people who know a lot about college basketball. They're former coaches, athletic directors, and administrators of the sport. They're educated people who should know what to emphasize at a particular point in time. In other words, they're not going to pick 20 at-large teams with losing records.

The year-over-year variance in the committee's output is shrinking as the process becomes more streamlined and more scrutinized. Some of the squirrely picks of yesteryear, which might have been unchallenged or unnoticed, are now going to get a full national laundering—and not just by me. I'm only one voice. You don't have to be a bracketologist to take issue with the committee. You basically have to be breathing.

Just as football fans can have an opinion on their team's pick in the NFL draft without ever seeing one minute of the guy's season at Running Back State, most basketball fans wouldn't know a team sheet if it came in the same envelope as their tax refund. It's sports, it's conjecture, it's water-cooler talk, it's opinion. And we're self-designated experts. I believe this level of interest and scrutiny has forced committee members to sharpen their pencils and up their games. The level of speculation is overwhelming—yes, I'm partly to blame—with both quantitative metrics and qualitative observation coloring the discussions. Anybody can watch any game in any part of the country live or taped. There's no under-the-radar team in Montana that only the committee knows about.

If 1979 repeated itself, we would see Indiana State and Larry Bird on national television 33 times instead of three. We'd at least have the ability to watch the non-televised games in some other way. I can't fault the cigar-smoking committee members of yesteryear for misevaluating a random mid-major when all they got were wire service leads and box scores. It's just a different time. I think the challenge now is in eliminating unnecessary information as opposed to assembling enough of it.

I am formulaic person. Therefore my evaluations are going to be mostly predictable and uniform. Yours may be more random. You might view the third-place team in the Big East way differently than the third-place team in the Pac-12 for no other reason than you have a different value system of what makes a team good. The only instructions given to the committee are to select the 36 best available at-large teams. It doesn't define best. It doesn't say most wins, highest NET, most Quad One wins, most deserving, toughest schedule, most NBA prospects, or brightest uniforms. (The latter would be Baylor, of course.) There is no official definition of best.

What we have are year-over-year outcomes, from which we can ascertain what the vast majority of committee members at the time defined as best. If they seeded the field in some future season by starting at NET 357 instead of NET 1, that would change things seismically—an extreme example, to be sure. But any changes force us to evaluate what they did and what they were thinking. That's why over the years I can make reasonably fact-based statements like "strength of schedule isn't as important as it used to be."

The weight of RPI in its later years as part of the overall decision-making process clearly declined. The number of at-large bids being awarded outside of major conferences has been going down dramatically. These are all quantifiable outcomes from which you can work backward to determine certain practices. What was the committee looking at to derive its results? Was it a fluke or a one-off? Is it something we should build into our evaluations going forward? By a little or by a lot?

Every seed list I do from November 15 to March 15 involves asking the question, "What's important to the committee this year?" And it's not just every time I do a seed list but every time I enter an individual team on the list. Theoretically, at least, I'm asking the question when distinguishing between teams one and two, then teams two and three, and so on. I do that every day and every night of every season. What's in my head on a given night, a given month, or a given year isn't the same as what it might have been on any date before. That is why we say Bracketology is an art *and* a science. The science is having the numbers; the art is applying them. And it is an ever-evolving art.

Picture the five Olympic rings. Let's say they represent the five most important metrics, and a couple of them are eye-test observations. Those rings aren't staying still. They're moving over and around each other all the time. The importance of ring No. 2 might be increasing this week because a bunch of bubble teams won big road games. And we might be influenced by that. Again, that's the human element, and the committee is made up of humans. If the team I'm advocating for to take the last at-large spot is No. 46 in the NET and the team you're advocating for is No. 48, that two-spot difference in their ranking doesn't mean a thing on the court. We're talking about wafer thin differences. If team No. 46 got to that point with two Quad One wins and team No. 48 has 10, I'm going to want to look deeper and know more. There's no way to put that into a single static formula. If there was, I wouldn't be up until 2:00 AM every night of the season. I would just run the numbers, wake up, and hit sort on my Excel sheet. Anybody can do that. Some people think that's all we do anyway. It's not, but you can't fight City Hall.

* * *

Over the years the influence of Bracketology among athletic directors, coaches, administrators, commissioners, and other people inside the sport definitely has grown. What used to be informal—like bumping into folks at a tournament, a press room, or an airport—has formalized to some degree in the last three to four years. I've twice been invited to the West Coast Conference coaches' meetings. I've been to the Atlantic 10 office, the Big East office, and the Pac-12 office. I have contacts at the SEC and the ACC—in part because ESPN has a partnership with those conferences and in part because of networks involved. I have good friends at the Missouri Valley Conference.

Through those conference-level consultations, there are now about a dozen schools I work with on a semi-formal basis in the offseason. Each spring I'll take a look at their non-conference commitments for the following year and suggest what they should be looking for if they consider themselves a serious at-large candidate. My response might be, "You're playing the equivalent of Kansas seven times. You better go get a couple of wins so you don't get fired."

More commonly, the schools that ask for my help tend to be aspirational. Kansas doesn't need my help to get a really good opponent. Generally speaking, if the Jayhawks want to play Michigan State or Duke, they're going to do it in the Champions Classic, in Maui, or wherever. Part of my work is to help identify in advance some under-the-radar opportunities for teams. And I do that with two conditions: I won't betray their confidence without permission by saying School A wanted to play School B but had to settle for

School C. In return, once the season starts, I have to be free to evaluate a team objectively. Just because we talked in June doesn't mean I'm going to like your profile in January. It can't work that way.

But even the best planning doesn't always play out. A team can play the right schedule and not win enough or it can win more than expected but play the wrong schedule. In other words, I could be wrong in forecasting schedule strength, or the team in question could underperform. Or both. Without naming names I worked very closely in the summer of 2019 with a mid-major that had at least one and maybe two recent seasons in which they were absolutely good enough for an at-large bid but played the wrong schedule and missed the NCAA field. After our offseason analysis, the same team won fewer games in 2019–20 than it had in the years it wasn't selected but was a likely single-digit seed had there been a 2020 tournament. The school was able to take an objective look at its data, which could have been provided by anyone. It just happened to be me in this case.

The flip side is that if you schedule for the NIT, you might get what you wished for. Oftentimes a school needs to take the chance of losing a couple more times to have an opportunity to win the *right* games. Part of my duties are to remind everyone involved that, "When the season starts, you're 0–0. You may like me now, but you may not like me in March."

Non-conference scheduling has evolved as much, if not more, than Bracketology. What do I mean by that? In the RPI era, which spans the majority of years I've been at this, schedule strength, and especially non-conference schedule strength, were huge and almost disproportionate components of the selection process. It came to be known—to some earlier than others and to almost everyone eventually—that scheduling practices could be manipulated to dramatically impact a team's RPI or Ratings Percentage Index. Using an example near and dear to my heart, Saint Joseph's was undefeated in the 2004 regular season and in contention for a No. 1 seed. The argument against the Hawks was, "You can't possibly be a No. 1 seed from a league like the Atlantic 10 when during the year you played only one ranked team."

St. Joe's opened that season with a win against Gonzaga—early in the Zags' time as a power—and never looked back. Gonzaga was its only ranked opponent. Yet the Hawks kept showing up with the nation's top RPI and No. 1 non-conference schedule—without playing in the ACC, without playing in the Big East, and without playing in the Big Ten. How did that happen?

I was working at St. Joe's at the time. Our schedule was built knowing we couldn't pick up the phone, call Duke, and schedule a game, but we could do so with Old Dominion. ODU winning 24 games would be almost as valuable in the RPI as Duke winning 26 games and had the added advantage that St. Joe's had a realistic chance to beat Old Dominion. In fact, Jameer Nelson hit a half-court shot, and the Hawks beat Old Dominion that year. It became a great win for RPI purposes. St. Joe's didn't play a losing team in the non-conference for the rest of the season and went into Selection Sunday with the No. 1 non-conference schedule in the country, essentially by targeting opponents' winning percentage regardless of conference affiliation. In other words, the Hawks couldn't eat at the same restaurant as Duke, but they could order the same steak at a lesser establishment, and it would still taste the same.

For 10 or 12 years after that, a lot of schools started to get wise to manipulating the RPI, even though I wasn't able to be in the business of helping them much. I had a real job after all. Then, before the 2018–19 season, the RPI went RIP, which was long overdue. With help from Google, the NCAA created NET as its new primary metric, creatively naming it the NCAA Evaluation Tool. They must have been up all night thinking of that one. We only have two years' worth of data with NET, but schedule strength seems to be diminishing as a factor in favor of team efficiency (offense and defense) and scoring margin. Whereas the RPI took three-fourths of its formula from who you played as opposed to wins and losses, NET measures *how* a team is playing—at least as much if not more than *who* it plays. Strength of schedule is now evaluated primarily by how your opponents break down across the four quads of the team sheet.

You'll hear people, including me, say, "That's a great Quad One win." Remember the quads operate on a sliding scale based on the location of the game. If a game is at home, it has to be against a Top 30 opponent to fall into the first quadrant. If at a neutral site, it needs to be against a Top 50 opponent, and a road game has to be against a Top 75 opponent. This system recognizes that it is at least twice as hard to win on the road. All of which is a major step forward. It also opens more possibilities when advising schools on scheduling. Let's call a school Hypothetical State. It's highly unlikely Hypo State can get a Power Five opponent to come to its campus. It's going to be tough to get any Top 30 team to Hypo State at its home unless it's a league game, which might happen occasionally but is not guaranteed in a mid-major conference.

The Atlantic 10, which is a step above mid-major status, isn't going to have a 2019–20 Dayton team every year. The Mountain West isn't going to have a 2019–20 San Diego State team every year. And the Missouri Valley isn't going to have Final Four-bound Loyola team every year, though

I'm told Sister Jean automatically improves their NET by 10 spots through divine intervention! What I would tell the AD at Hypothetical State is, if they're not in a conference which guarantees you a high number of Quad One games, they've got to be really creative in that category. It could be via inclusion in a strong multi-team event (MTE) or creating opportunities for high-end neutral court games. Somebody has to fill out the field in the Paradise Jam and the tournaments in Orlando, Florida, or Charleston or Myrtle Beach, South Carolina. Those events can't include only top 10 teams. A school in the middle of a power conference or at the top of a mid-major league can get multiple high-value games from a good MTE.

We've also seen conferences outside the Power Five pair up. The Atlantic 10 and Mountain West have begun a challenge. San Diego State was scheduled to play at Saint Louis as part of the 2020–21 event before the pandemic intervened. The Aztecs were coming off a historic season, and the Billikens were set to be picked first or second in the A-10. This is extremely smart scheduling. You might have to leave home, which a lot of schools don't want to do because they lose gate, and it's certainly harder to win. But the smarter ones realize beating East Armpit State at home doesn't help, at least if you do it too many times. It's one thing to have a couple of those games per year. It's another to have it be the bulk of your non-conference schedule.

A team can be 28–6, but if a third or more of those wins are schools in the 300s, it doesn't help (and can even hurt) your postseason chances. Who have you beaten that would be comparable to a team you might play in the NCAA Tournament? That's what it all comes down to. In the tournament you're going to play mostly Top 50 teams on a neutral court. That's what Quad One is trying to replicate. Serious contenders need to play enough of those games for the committee to make a proper evaluation. We know from two years of NET data that the average NCAA at-large team—outside of the Power Five and the Big East—plays a half dozen Quad One games. If you're not in one of those conferences, you've got to go get them somehow, some way. It could mean traveling, it could mean being bought, it could mean neutral-site matchmaker games.

In November of 2019, I finished broadcasting my opening night assignment at Saint Joseph's. When I came home and turned on the television, not only was the Champions Classic on, but Wisconsin was also playing St. Mary's somewhere in South Dakota. You might say to yourself, *Why?* Well, many of these matchups are promoted with TV in mind. Beyond that, Wisconsin knows it's going to have a ton of hard Big Ten games, but the Badgers don't want all of their non-league games to be homecourt cupcakes. St. Mary's gave them a good opponent without going across the country.

The Gaels could forget about getting Wisconsin to come to Moraga, California. There isn't a guarantee big enough for that. So it's worth the trip to South Dakota. Heck, it would have been worth going to the South Pole after St. Mary's won in overtime. And the loss didn't really hurt Wisconsin because the Gaels were a likely NCAA team. Everybody wins.

* * *

I get a bit of friendly feedback every year. Toward the end of the 2019–20 season, there was a Bracketology firestorm involving Indiana coach Archie Miller. Following a tough home loss to Wisconsin, Miller was asked about the Hoosiers' possible "Last Four In" status. At the time I was 700 miles away in Philadelphia, but that didn't stop Coach Miller from going off and saying something about stuffing me in a trash can like Oscar the Grouch.

Other than calling me the wrong *Sesame Street* character—I'm more the Cookie Monster type—Miller was absolutely on point to lobby for his team. And I was perfectly on point to question Indiana's resume and evaluate the Hoosiers accordingly. Miller's problem was that the cameras were on, and his tantrum made the news. He may have been right. Maybe the Hoosiers deserved better than Last Four In status. The season wasn't over, the Big Ten Tournament had yet to be played, and there were countless possibilities out there for IU. Interestingly, during the offseason I conducted four mock selection exercises for hardcore fans around the country, re-starting the conference tournaments where we left off on the Thursday of Championship Week. Indiana made the field in all of them, and in all but one, the Hoosiers were the Last Four In.

Feedback and criticism are now instantaneous across the board. When Bracketology began, the most common methods were direct emails. People would look me up on the Saint Joseph's University website and let me know *exactly* what they were thinking. Or I would do online chat sessions every week on ESPN.com. Today we call them social media takeovers. Anyone could go to a common site and ask a question. At its peak I would get more than 500 questions in an hour and answer 20 or 30, typing responses as fast as I could.

Today's equivalent is texting or a tweet. It's just the cost of doing business. If game announcers are going to say during every key broadcast from early February to the end of the season, "Here's where Joe Lunardi has these teams," viewers are going to react. If it was my team, I would react. I can't bite the hand that feeds me and criticize fans for being fans, especially when the goal of our enterprise is to engage them. I want to be out there giving the most pertinent opinion every day on every team in the country, and it'd be great if their fans always smiled and said, "Thank you, sir, may I have another?" But that's just not realistic.

It's good news to have nearly a quarter-million Twitter followers. The bad news is I've got nearly a quarter-million Twitter followers who may not agree with me. I don't do the ESPN chat rooms anymore. They no longer exist. So once or twice a week, as I'm watching a game at home, I might take to Twitter and offer a few insights. It's like lighting a fuse. I know the feedback is coming. That's okay. I mostly like it. It's an opportunity to speak directly to fans and maybe learn some things along the way.

Of course, I like to think the brevity of Twitter plays to my rapier wit. I'm never afraid to throw out a zinger and have a little fun. It's like going to a sports bar without leaving the sofa. I feel the same way walking into a game. When I'm in an arena outside the Philly area and fans call out to me, I'm good with it whether it's a positive or negative reaction. If I wanted to be anonymous, I could stay home and watch the game on television. That wouldn't be as much fun.

I'm reminded every day that the word *fan* is short for *fanatic*. It has dual connotations. It could mean: that person is serious about college basketball. *He's a fanatic.* Or it could mean: that person is way over the top. *He's a fanatic.* Both reactions are part of the deal. People in the public eye often say they don't they read what others write about them or pay attention to what others are saying about them. At least 99 percent of those public figures are lying. We all pay attention because it's human nature. To whatever degree I am a public figure, I pay attention and try to be reasonably responsive to it. It's a matter of degree.

I remember a great quote from years and years ago and I use it all the time. Dick Vermeil was the new head coach in Philadelphia, and the Eagles were terrible. He had to pick a quarterback. Vermeil picked one guy (Ron Jaworski), but the fans liked another one (Roman Gabriel). It was the classic case of the backup quarterback being the most popular guy in town. Vermeil said, "You can listen to the fans in the 700 level if you want. But if you do, pretty soon you'll be sitting with them."

I listen to what coaches and fans and other media say about their teams, but it's up to me whether or not to take it seriously. It's dishonest to say I don't hear it. What's more honest is to say I hear almost everything. I just don't apply it or take it seriously very often. The closer it gets to Selection

Sunday, the less I read, listen, hear, or allow into my tiny little brain. I have a process that's been reasonably successful. Even though I may tweak it year to year or even within a given season, that process shouldn't be unduly influenced by outside chatter any more than the 10 people on the committee reading the newspaper or listening to TV commentators.

The committee members are supposed to be sequestered. If they're sequestered, I should be, too, because fundamentally I'm trying to replicate their process to the greatest degree possible. Every step I take away from that is placing me closer to the fan and further from the committee itself. I'll have a chance to be a fan soon enough.

CHAPTER SIX

Debunking the Myths

P erhaps the most common Bracketology myth is that the Selection Committee wants to see rivals, who won't schedule each other during the regular season, play in their tournament. Think Kansas vs. Missouri, Texas vs. Texas A&M, or a current rivalry that wasn't played for years like Kentucky vs. Louisville. I don't know what it was like in the really old days before the 64-team field came into existence. There's not much of a historical record of the committee process from those years, and there was certainly no Selection Show. The athletic director got a call from somebody saying his school was in the NCAA Tournament, playing so-and-so at fill-in-the-blank arena. If the team won, it advanced, and someone informed the school who it was playing next.

That's pretty much how the NIT was administered until the NCAA took it over in 2005 and gave it a bracket of its own. Before that the NIT process was literally: let's see who wins and figure out the best matchups for the next round. It wasn't even seeded. It was kind of based on geography. And gate appeal was paramount as an attempt to get the most attractive teams to Madison Square Garden.

Before the regions were balanced in the NCAA Tournament, geography ruled the pairings. Teams that played during the season would be matched up if it made sense. In some cases close rivals were matched to sell more tickets. Competing with the NIT was also an issue along with media coverage. Most of the coverage of the early tournaments was nuts-and-bolts stuff, featuring game stories and not much analysis. Nobody would have thought to ask in, say, 1958 why Oklahoma State was paired with who-knows-who. It just wasn't thought about, at least not in a broad way. You played who it made sense to play, where it was most convenient, and that was that.

I remember in 1983 when Louisville and Kentucky were first matched up in the tournament. The schools hadn't met since 1959, but they didn't have a choice. The NCAA forced their hand, and everyone lived to see another day. And the two programs began to realize it was good for business to renew a series—even if they claimed to loathe each other.

Regardless, once the field expanded and the teams were seeded in each region—not to mention the committee's power to send any school to any region in the country to balance the bracket—the NCAA pairings ceased to be about storylines. Of course, when we look at a bracket—even my mocks—there are always "I see what you did there" comments. But I haven't done anything intentionally, nor does the committee, when implementing its numerous principles and procedures. Someone will write to me and say something like, "You have Seton Hall playing Louisville. That's Kevin Willard against where his dad was Rick Pitino's assistant." Well, I actually didn't think of that. I was probably just trying to make the seeds line up correctly or avoid having a Big East team slotted in a sub-regional where it can't go. Or keep Louisville from the KFC Yum! Center, its home arena, in a year where it's a host institution.

Over the years the committee has added more bracketing rules, not less. So the notion of trying to make Kansas play Missouri in a possible No. 1 vs. No. 8 game in the second round is pretty ridiculous. For every reason you might want it to happen, there could be more procedural reasons why it can't. Look at it another way. Think of all the possible rivalries that *haven't* been arranged by the NCAA. When Xavier went to the Big East, the Musketeers decided not to play Dayton anymore. That was an annual rivalry game, and there are so many others. UConn and UMass had something going for a few years, but they stopped playing. Boston College won't play UMass either. The same goes with Georgetown and Maryland in D.C. For years John Thompson wanted no part of local rivalries.

It's hard enough to follow all the bracketing rules without manipulating matchups. If you try to manipulate, you're almost invariably going to break some of the committee's rules. I would say to the average fan—whatever you think you know and I'm talking about bracketing and pairings not selection and seeding here—you're probably wrong. This proves itself every time I've taught Fundamentals of Bracketology as a class either online or at Saint Joseph's University. My students, who are bright, hard-core fans, realize there are only so many ways to place their seed list onto an empty bracket sheet.

Bracketology, at least the science of it, helps to bridge this gap. In laying out all the data, some matchups simply fall into place. Having said that, I think a little more common sense could be applied to bracketing at times, cutting down on travel and adding interest without compromising balance. But at the end of the day, all the tickets are pretty much sold, so it's not about gate. It's also not about ratings because the television contract is signed years out, and that money is guaranteed. An argument could be made that if the TV ratings dramatically tank, the next rights renewal would be significantly reduced. My answer to that is, "I'll believe it when it happens."

Another thing to consider: is Kansas vs. Missouri going to drive up ratings anywhere but those states, where fans are going to tune in regardless of who their teams play? No. We're not talking North Carolina and Duke, *who have never met in the tournament.* That will happen someday, by the way, most likely very deep in the tourney. There have already been Final Fours featuring both schools, but their regions didn't connect. Whenever it happens, it will be a ratings bonanza.

One of the most exciting championship games ever was in 2010 when Duke beat Butler. Butler's Gordon Hayward hit the rim from half court at the final buzzer. Had it gone in, the Bulldogs would have won the whole thing. But no one said ahead of time, "That would be a great final. It's a great matchup." Yet it was inches from being the greatest ending in the history of sports.

All the tickets are pretty much sold before the pairings are announced. The rights fees are negotiated years in advance. There are 67 total games in the tournament. You can't help but get every type and size of market, historical storylines, and just plain drama. No one ever calls it March Meh.

Team selection and bracketing should be as neutral and sterile an enterprise as possible, leading to the fewest competitive advantages for anyone. When No. 9 seed Northern Iowa took the court against No. 1 overall seed Kansas in Oklahoma City in 2010, the Panthers should have had as fair a chance as the Jayhawks. Obviously, Kansas has more highly regarded players. Bracketing isn't ever going to change that, nor should it. But the bracketing rules for the most part are designed so that when the pregame clock hits zero and the ball goes up, nobody has a head start. This concept now includes a prohibition of playing on your home court.

I don't know the last time somebody hosted a tournament game in the main bracket. I do remember being in the Carrier Dome when Syracuse lost to David Robinson and Navy in 1986. That was a huge deal. When Villanova won its first title in 1985, the first year of the 64-team field, the Wildcats played an No. 8 vs. No. 9 game against Dayton at the UD Arena. They won 51–49 to start their run. Dayton also played a home game in 2015 in the First Four, the last time it happened for anyone because the Flyers were one of the last four at-large teams. That was unavoidable.

Most of these rules have been made to provide the fairest competition possible and avoid rematches, especially among teams from the same conference. One of the things that made Major League Baseball cool before 1994 was that the teams from the National League and the American League never played each other except in the World Series (or maybe spring training). That has been eroded over time. Interleague play was a big deal when it first started, but now there's an interleague game every night because both leagues have an odd number of teams.

Another myth is the supposed desire of the committee to match up coaches with their former schools. It does happen but not by design. Coaches move around a lot, but today's players move around even more. In a year or two, nobody will pay as much attention to coaches meeting their former teams as they will players competing against former teammates. What was once the coaching carousel could soon be more like the point-guard carousel. The growing number of transfers may be good for the players, but it could hurt the sport. Taking it to the extreme, if unlimited transfers happen with no exceptions, a guy could play for four teams in four years. However unlikely that is, it would be very hard for fans to identify with teams in such a scenario. I can almost hear John Wooden say to Bill Walton, "Son, you are more than welcome to transfer to Grateful Dead State. Make sure to drop off your playbook with my assistant."

But fans will always—*always*—identify with the NCAA Tournament, and for pretty much the opposite reason, they watch the other major sports. We cherish the unpredictability. In baseball when the New York Yankees win, the ratings go up. In basketball when "the Butler does it," the ratings go up. And Butler is closer to being the Kansas City Royals than the Yankees. I'm not saying the networks don't like Duke, Kentucky, and Kansas. They do. But look at how much excitement was generated and ultimately lost in the 2020 tournament with Dayton and San Diego State as potential No. 1 seeds. When George Mason, VCU, and

Loyola Chicago made the Final Four in recent years, the excitement was off the charts. And I suspect the amount of unpredictability is enhanced by the lack of bracket manipulation. I know I'm in the minority on this. Most people, even the most grizzled observers of the tournament (media and otherwise), believe there is a certain amount of matchmaking taking place. But it's the organic unpredictability that creates the most excitement. It can't be scripted.

Just like trying to force-feed rivalries, forcing coaches to play their former teams is not worth the trouble. There are too many other factors that go into bracketing and seeding without trying to script something unnatural. And remember: the only certain pairings are the first-round games. We may look ahead to great storylines in the later rounds, but the round orange ball rarely bounces as planned. UMBC anyone?

Another myth is putting undeserving teams in the tournament strictly because of star power. Does the committee look past a substandard resumé to make sure a marquee player is in the field? I don't believe they do and I can provide very recent examples. I'm a Philadelphia 76ers fan. The Sixers have had two No. 1 overall picks in the past few years, presumably the best players in college from each of those drafts—Ben Simmons and Markelle Fultz. Neither made the tournament during their one year in college. So it happened twice in three years that the best player in the nation didn't play in the NCAA Tournament. One could argue that LSU (Simmons) and Washington (Fultz) weren't anywhere close to the bubble during the seasons in question. They weren't crawling across the bottom of the screen as part of the First Four Out. But the committee's only job is to select the best teams. There's no way they add player personnel and scouting to a job description that already has more regulations than the IRS code.

What about the human element? The most recent example is probably Trae Young at Oklahoma in 2018. The Sooners had a terrific non-conference season. Young was going off seemingly every night. Then Oklahoma got into league play, particularly the back half of the Big 12 schedule, and it was losing regularly. The Sooners finished with a losing record in the conference after a poor six- or eight-week stretch. When they made the field, they weren't even among the last at-large teams. They were a No. 10 seed, losing to Rhode Island in overtime. Although most presumed Oklahoma would be chosen mainly because of Young, I made a different argument: "There's no doubt in my mind Oklahoma will make it, but it's because they have so many Quad One wins." Their selection didn't have anything to do with Young, at least beyond his on-court contributions to those victories.

Full disclosure: if I was on the committee that year, I would not have voted for Oklahoma. Knowing the Sooners would make it is different from supporting their inclusion. I would have applied the "Lunardi Rule" prohibiting sub-.500 conference teams, but that's another topic for a later chapter. The Sooners made the 2018 tourney with an 8–10 conference record and the 2019 tourney with a 7–11 conference record. That's two at-large bids for a team that was a combined six games below .500 in its own league. Nothing at all against Oklahoma, but that's outrageous.

For the most part, you'd be hard pressed to find comparable Young examples. This is not to shill for the committee or to defend them; my job is just the opposite most of the time. Teams with multiple great wins make the tournament far more often than not. Put enough notches in your belt and you'll get an invite to the dance even if, as in Oklahoma's case, your pants are falling down at the end of the season. But let's say it came down to Oklahoma and St. Bonaventure for the very last spot. Is it possible the committee members are more likely to press for Oklahoma than the Bonnies because Young was talked about on ESPN every 15 minutes for four months. For the same reason, Syracuse might get in over St. Bonaventure.

Historically, team appeal is a far greater factor than player appeal. It's easy to find the numbers to back up any argument, even more so for perennial NCAA participants. It's the same reason people buy Xerox machines instead of

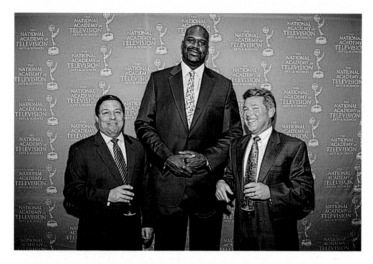

Bracketology meets Shaq-a-tology, along with ESPN producer Jim Bowdon, at the 2012 Sports Emmy Awards. *(Courtesy Jim Bowdon)*

I'm with Tacko Fall at the Charleston Classic in 2018. One of us is among the 40 tallest people on Earth. *(Courtesy Chris Farrow)*

I work *The Bracketology Show* on ESPN+ with Sean Farnham. It launched in January of 2020. *(Courtesy Tim Dwyer)*

I give legendary announcer Bill Raftery a few pointers at Villanova University in 2016.
(Courtesy Matt Martucci)

At the 2016 East Regional in Philadelphia, I make a belated case for St. Bonaventure
to Selection Committee chair Joe Castiglione and longtime ESPN colleague Andy Katz.
(Courtesy Joe Lunardi)

I'm inside the Bracket Bunker with ESPN's Phil Skender, the man who makes it shine, in 2020. *(Courtesy Joe Lunardi)*

I work The Basketball Tournament at Thomas Jefferson University in Philadelphia with Matt Martucci (right) and Nick Elam, the innovator behind the "Elam Ending." *(Courtesy Joe Lunardi)*

I can score a 68 in Bracketology but not golf—except for my "One Shining Moment" at Llanerch Country Club in June of 2013. I aced the 157-yard 12th hole with friends John McGeever, Marty Farrell, and then-Saint Joseph's coach Phil Martelli. *(Courtesy Martin Farrell)*

At Lahinch Golf Club in Ireland in May of 2017, I was told: "There are two goats on the course; the white one is friendly." *(Courtesy Rob DeLong)*

I work on this book with my coauthor David Smale in Lenexa, Kansas.
(Courtesy David Smale)

From left to right, the First Family of Bracketology: Lizzy, Emily, and wife Pam break bread with me. *(Courtesy Joe Lunardi)*

Brand X copy products. We default to the familiar. This human element is an assumed risk of the process, but we still need it in the room—as opposed to a Bowl Championship Series-like formula—to spot outliers and apply common sense. Like referees, committee members get it mostly right anyway.

But regarding star power, I've heard every committee chair explain every bubble pick for more than 20 years. I've heard a lot of good reasons and I've heard more than my share of cockamamie reasons. I've never heard marquee appeal of star players as a reason to select or seed a team. For the NIT? Absolutely, particularly in the old days when it was a gate event as opposed to a bracketed event. It's an invitational after all. Similarly, Tiger Woods will be at The Masters in 20 years even if he's not one of the top 50 players in the world. The Masters is an invitational. The NCAA Tournament is the U.S. Open. It is an earned, championship event.

* * *

Maybe we've all watched too many old movies like *12 Angry Men*, but many people think the committee room is the scene of frequent dustups. I'm sure it can be contentious at times, as a member could be passionate in advocating for or against a team he or she was monitoring during the season. But there are no fights, shouts, or fisticuffs. Maybe in the old days, when the good ol' boys smoked cigars while representing their own leagues, there could have been scenes like that. And I'm sure there was some horse trading, too. *I don't think Kansas State deserves to make the field, but I'll put them in if you let me have Iowa.* We talk about the human element, so we have to assume the tournament bigwigs of yore acted the part. I would love to be able to go back in time and interview men like Walter Byers and Wayne Duke. Maybe they took some funny business to their graves, and maybe that's not a bad thing.

Today's committee room is too organized and structured for funny business. For one, when a team from a representative's conference—especially their own school—is being discussed, they must recuse themselves. *Recuse* doesn't mean merely leaving the room. At my first media mock exercise, I was representing Mike Slive, the late SEC commissioner. Whenever a discussion or a vote came up that involved an SEC team, my computer would lock. I couldn't even look at the data, much less vote. If it's just a procedural thing, you can sit there quietly. But if a serious discussion ensues, you go to next room and enjoy the snacks! Eventually, they let you back in the room.

What kind of informal conversations occur over coffee or other beverages? Who knows. Only so much discussion can be restricted. Let's say you're a committee member and athletic director for St. Bonaventure, and your team was just voted out of the field. You may not have been part of the discussion, but you're going to know what the other nine people just did when you come back. There's no hiding the fact that Syracuse is on the board, and your team isn't.

At that point the expectation is that you grit your teeth, say "that sucks," and maybe ask a question or two. The chair or an NCAA staffer then says, "We need to move on now." And just like the best referees on the court, the best committee members move on to the next play. I recall a year when Mike Tranghese, the Big East commissioner, was a veteran committee member, and the Atlantic 10 got one more bid than the Big East. After the fact some of the Big East coaches went after their own commissioner, questioning, "What good are you if that can happen?"

Tranghese basically responded, "I'm not in the room at the time."

Over a cup of coffee or a bagel in the morning, does a good commissioner go up to his or her fellow members and say, "I want to make sure you have all the information you need on my teams." I assume this takes place and I don't have any problem with it. It's human nature; otherwise, we're sending 10 robots. But when it comes time to vote, we want the dads who coach their own kids in Little

League. He's harder on his own son or daughter than he is on the rest of the team. I've done the mocks multiple times. One year St. Joe's was right on the bubble, and I was in the room. I wasn't representing St. Joe's or the Atlantic 10, so I could theoretically advocate on their behalf. Instead I tried extra hard not to speak beyond the data—and I'm just their radio guy!

In my experience the vast majority of committee members go out of their way to be fair-minded. But just as it is perfectly human to be influenced by brand names and star power, there's a human element to want to be liked and approved. In this case that's getting the selections and seeding right. The cacophony of critics, myself included, can get pretty nasty (and some are *way* over the top). I find my own worst moments come right after the selections are announced and I haven't slept. I've been known to write or say one or two things that were regrettable. That's my human element, and the main reason I prefer not to go on the air right after the Selection Show. It's better to take a breath and look at the results more objectively.

The process is skewed to the power conferences and the football schools. There is no debating that. There is also no debating that over the last decade or two the number of at-large bids awarded to so-called "mid majors" is going down. That's not because of the 10 people in the room. That's because of the politics of the sport. Before those 10 people even get in the room, it's been determined that about half the committee is composed of power conference representatives. It's in the bylaws. The big boys have half the votes before they open the polls. Irrespective of the inherent advantage of being one of those schools in the first place, which you generally earned by investing in intercollegiate athletics at an incredibly high level, 10 people can't undo the economic and demographic realities of the sport. There will always be a nexus of debate between the haves and the have-nots just as in almost every other endeavor since the beginning of time.

* * *

Another major myth pertains to the number of teams selected from a conference. Beyond the automatic qualifiers, there is neither a maximum nor a minimum. It's the first sentence on the principles and procedures document and has been for a long time, which reads: "The committee shall select the 36 best at-large teams, regardless of conference affiliation."

It has become part of the language in recent years for committee members to say (and you can believe this to whatever degree you wish): "We view every team as an independent and every game as its own entity." The reality is that if a school happens to be in the Atlantic Coast Conference, 20 of its data points are ACC games. Ninety-nine times out of a hundred, that's going to put an ACC school's resume way ahead of one from the Atlantic Sun Conference.

Can a really good Atlantic Sun team close the gap by scheduling and playing up in the other third of its season? Yes, but it will never close the gap entirely. This was part of the story in the famed 1966 championship game between Kentucky against Texas Western. Forget the enormous racial implications for a minute. The bluest of the blue bloods lost to a little-known mid-major. Texas Western wasn't even UTEP yet, making its title even more significant. Go to the head of the class if you can even name Texas Western's conference at that time.

Whenever I do a mock bracket, I count up how many teams are included from each conference. The totals are listed on ESPN.com's Bracketology page as a news item, but there is no comparable exercise by the committee. Conference affiliation isn't on the team sheets, and no tally of conference members is kept as teams are voted into or out of the field. In 2019–20 one of my in-season bracket updates included a dozen Big Ten teams. That would be a record for a single conference. Part of me said, "This isn't happening in real life." The reason it wouldn't happen has nothing to do with the committee being afraid to do so. The reason is that for this particular bracket in January the Big Ten bubble teams hadn't played each other enough to knock themselves out of consideration. And the conference tournament hadn't taken place, which might have presented one or more pseudo-elimination games. Timing is critical to Bracketology.

When the committee is voting—let's say Indiana and East Tennessee State are in contention for a No. 9 seed—the members might look at each team sheet side by side. The top of ETSU would read: "East Tennessee State, 30–4" followed by the remainder of its data and quad breakdown. It doesn't read: "East Tennessee State, Southern Conference." Neither conference name nor conference record are included, though I believe the latter is significantly undervalued. Indiana and its 20–12 overall record would read similarly. Nowhere is it indicated that "nine Big Ten teams have already been voted into the field." A member could look up at the board and count in his or her head, but no written numerical record of that exists. So conversations on the order of, say, "the SEC is a six-bid league," are completely moot.

Conference membership does come into play on the bracketing side. There are principles on the rounds in which teams from the same conference can have rematches from the regular season or their conference tournament. Another conference-related principle comes into play at the top of the bracket. Teams from the same conference that are seeded on the top four lines have to be in separate regions. Let's say the Big Ten has a No. 1, No. 2, No. 3, and No. 4 seed among its entries. One each will be in the East, South, Midwest, and West. If any conference has a fifth team among the top four seeds, as was the case with the ACC and Virginia Tech in 2019, then some doubling up is necessary. But the idea is to keep the very best teams in any league from knocking each other out.

It used to be that the first three teams selected from any league, no matter their seeding, had to be in different regions. Then the committee realized it was restricting itself for little gain. What if two teams from the Atlantic 10 were a No. 9 seed and a No. 11 seed? The chances of them meeting before the regional final is pretty remote, so why ship a team from its natural region? When was the last time an Elite Eight game took place between a 9-seed and an 11-seed?

Oh, yeah, No. 9 Kansas State vs. No. 11 Loyola Chicago in 2018. Good thing they weren't in the same conference.

The final bracketing principle revolves around the definition of a home court. The rule states a team can't compete at any site at which it played more than three regular-season games. Villanova has strategically cut back on its use of the Wells Fargo Center, home of the Philadelphia 76ers, so it can play first- and second-round NCAA games in its own backyard. Same for Kansas at the T-Mobile Center in Kansas City, Missouri, which often hosts the Big 12 Tournament. (It's fortunate for the Jayhawks that conference tourney games don't count.) There are a few quirky rules like that. Extra quirky is BYU's restriction on Sunday sports, which has caused its share of headaches on multiple occasions.

One final pet peeve: the vast majority of the committee's time is spent on selection and seeding—day after day, hour after hour, game after game. There have been years when the actual bracket released to CBS is completed right up against the Selection Show deadline, distilling five days of haggling into a 45-minute burst. The committee should have more time to step back and look at the bracket in total, anticipating issues beyond the first round in terms of fairness, balance, geography, or whatever. A common refrain from past committee members—"You can play your way out of a bad seed or a bad pairing, but you can't play your way out if you're not in the field at all"—is beside the point. They should get selections right. And seeding. And pairings.

The majority of teams are solidly in the field either as an automatic qualifier or selected at-large without much dissent. It makes no sense, though, for those teams to be haphazardly placed because the committee is in a hurry. Let's take one last look at, say, Arizona State being in Albany, New York, and Providence in San Jose, California, as No. 7

seeds. Maybe we can do better. With a little more time on Selection Sunday—ideally with all conference tourney games concluding on Saturday—the committee might identify an instance or two in which it could move one domino and make it better for five others. Instead, the time crunch and bracketing rules prevent this kind of tweaking. Once the bracketing begins, they simply go down the seed list one by one. If something with team No. 27 messes up the placement of the next eight teams, tough luck. But maybe something could have been done with team No. 26 to keep any of the dominoes from falling. If the field was completely set by Saturday night, the committee would have all of Sunday to build the perfect bracket. Of course, we would still pick it apart.

CHAPTER SEVEN

A Language
All Its Own

There are quite a few unique terms associated with Bracketology. Some of them originated elsewhere, but many were born right here. Let's start with the term *Bracketology* itself. Mike Jensen of *The Philadelphia Inquirer* referenced the term way back in 1996.

We may never know who first thought up Bracketology, but I remember exactly where I was when I first heard the word *bracketologist*. I was at St. Bonaventure's Reilly Center in late February, standing on the court after a game between Saint Joseph's and the Bonnies. My cell phone rang, and it was Jensen calling from back in Philadelphia. At that time he was the Temple beat writer on his way to becoming the paper's college columnist. He was doing a recap of the Philly-area schools and their respective chances to make the NCAA Tournament. His main question was something on the order of where Temple stood. Some thought Temple was a bubble team at that point, but I felt like the Owls were solidly in that year's field. In his reporting Jensen said I referred to myself as a "bracketologist." So be it. It wasn't long before bracketologist (little b) morphed into Bracketology (capital B). It was a breakthrough of sorts.

Memories are fuzzy, but ESPN.com was already giving the brackets some in-season attention. The great Howie Schwab was formulating his own projections of the field, maybe even calling it Bracketology, though he doesn't remember for sure. "But it really took off with Joe," Schwab said.

Schwab was great to me when I started with ESPN.com. He was an early editor of the brackets and very supportive of my efforts, even though he may have been first to the starting line. "I'm thrilled that he turned this into a career," Schwab said. "A lot of people do it now, but everybody knows who Joe Lunardi is. Some coaches hate his guts, but it's an inexact science, and Joe is one of the best. It didn't take long [for Bracketology] to be embraced."

Rightly or wrongly, others began to associate me with the concept and the label. There were more spin-offs. Nike ran tournament commercials using the theme "Bracketville." Folks in the media and elsewhere started bracketing non-basketball things. The New York Times writer Richard Sandomir wrote a book called The Enlightened Bracketologist. It was comprised of lists and rankings of things—like the best candy bar or the best comic strips—that didn't have anything to do with the NCAA Tournament. I was never particularly good at the business of business, so I never made any attempt to copyright or trademark any of my Bracketology work. Other sports figures were making hay in that area with terms like "three-peat" (Pat Riley) and "Refuse to Lose" (John Calipari). In my world two things were working against any bracket-related trademarks.

One was that the term itself Bracketology was considered to be in the public domain and therefore unable to be secured by a single party. It would have been like trying to trademark the word *computer*. The other reason is ESPN's ownership rights for anything appearing on its platforms. What the network airs, it owns. And I never gave it another serious thought. "Joe was very smart," Jensen said while becoming one of the few people to ever call me "smart" in public. "I asked him after he went to ESPN if he had tried to copyright [the term]. He said 'No,' which was the smartest thing he ever did. If he had, ESPN could have said, 'Congratulations, Mr. Bracketologist, you can have a nice little website called Bracketology.com, and we'll hire whomever and call it something else.' Instead Bracketology became his without him needing to copyright anything, and he's made out fine. ESPN could have had issues. Instead, they branded him the bracketologist. Without that branding it wouldn't have been the same."

Obviously, there were brackets for athletic competitions all over the world long before I came along—from the famed high school basketball tournament in Indiana to the FIFA

World Cup. I didn't come close to inventing brackets as a way of arranging championships. As far as copyrights are concerned, as long as I can use Bracketology, we're good. And ESPN has given me everything I could have wanted in the way of exposure and editorial freedom. Any Bracketology-related search is going to include me as a primary source, and that's more than enough. We're not talking about the polio—or coronavirus—vaccine. I was just having fun with basketball. Being the first bracketologist was a hobby. I had another profession at the time and never envisioned working in college basketball to this extent. Besides, if anyone ever asks, I'm the one with a letter from the *Oxford English Dictionary* for creating a word.

Bracketology belongs to everyone in our great game. I'd have to be pretty greedy, selfish, and narrow-minded to think something that clearly belongs to millions of people could be mine alone. If not for those millions of fans, nobody would care. It's not that I don't have an ego, it's that I was raised to value a greater good and hope to provide that example for my own family.

Plenty of people already say Joe Lunardi and Bracketology have become part of the fabric of college basketball. What could be better than that? I can't play or coach a lick, which is well-documented, so it's crazy to think basketball could be in the first paragraph of my obituary. I might prefer it to read: "Joe Lunardi, whose memorable hole-in-one in June 2013 propelled him..." But that's not going first. I'd even settle for "a loving husband and father of two," but we all know the word Bracketology will be right at the top. There are a lot worse things to be known for.

One of the terms most associated with Bracketology is *bubble* (long before it became part of the coronavirus lexicon). The bubble also preceded me in terms of its use for teams at selection time. Having said that, I don't think it preceded me by much because the public nature of the selection process doesn't predate me by very much. There were bubble teams as soon as the limit of teams from a single conference was removed. I used the term from the beginning. I was probably taking the term from ESPN or other media covering college basketball at the time. There were always debates about whether or not a team would get in. I covered a Villanova team in 1990–91 that received an at-large bid despite having a 16–14 record and being just 7–9 in the Big East. At the time it was the worst overall record for an at-large team. Did anybody call those Wildcats a bubble team? Quite likely.

If memory serves, it was even more common to say certain teams were "on the bubble." I probably had something to do with the subtle shift in language from on the bubble to "bubble team" because using that term is more unique to uncovering the process than the term "on the bubble." The official NCAA term is "under consideration," which isn't sexy enough for a halftime show. In the earliest days of the Selection Committee, its members would often speak of something called the *consideration board*. If that brings to your mind images of flip charts and easels, you're not alone. Today teams get voted into or out of the at-large pool from a digital under consideration list. It's part of the laptop software each committee member has for the selection meeting. To even be discussed, a team must first receive multiple votes to join the under consideration list. At one time teams went on the consideration board automatically as a regular-season or division champion in their conference. When I talk today about not paying enough attention to regular-season champions, I'm referring to a mostly bygone period when it was a formal part of the process.

To my way of thinking, this is a significant and erroneous omission. Regular-season conference championships or even divisional titles are legitimate evaluation criteria. Just like my Philadelphia Eagles won the NFC East in 2019 at 9–7 and earned a home playoff game against a wild-card team with a better record. The Eagles *won something* the NFL deems valuable. The Selection Committee should re-emphasize a similar practice.

The bubble can also be fun. I remember an early *SportsCenter* segment when Linda Cohn was the anchor. It was a Sunday morning, and she suggested we play Lawrence Welk music. The producers went one better and delivered a bubble machine for that part of the show. Somewhere, my Grandmom Ciccantelli—who made us watch Lawrence Welk as kids—was smiling. Other times we would blow up balloons and put bubble team logos on them. The director had me pop the bubbles of teams I didn't think would make the field. Somehow this qualified as riveting television.

A couple of terms I definitely invented were *Last Four In* and *First Four Out*. I wasn't trying to be creative but was simply representing the process the committee goes through. Then and now, the committee frequently evaluates and votes teams into the field—or seeds teams—four at a time. The process begins on the Wednesday of Championship Week with each of the 10 committee members listing up to 36 teams they feel should be in the tournament regardless of pending results in the various conference tournaments. In other words, these are the locks. If a team receives a designated number of votes in this initial balloting, it goes into the at-large field. Teams receiving multiple votes but less than the designated number go on the aforementioned under consideration list. Typically, there are between 20 to 25 locks after initial balloting. Many will become AQs (automatic qualifiers) as the conference tourneys play out, meaning the number of additional at-large teams needed to reach the eventual total of 36 is fluid. The committee is continually evaluating teams on the "under consideration" list and will seed teams all weekend on the at-large list.

The most common voting practice is known as *list eight, rank four*, in which a ballot of eight teams is identified from the list in question, and the top four teams are selected from that ballot via a 1–8 ranking. The easiest way for the public to understand this process is through our Four In, Four Out vocabulary. With every ballot, be it a selection or seeding vote, teams 1–4 are slotted, and teams 5–8 go back on the list for further review. I've always viewed the "Last Four In" as replicating the final ballot, though the number could be less than four when the very last vote takes place. But the concept—the Last Four In are the at-large teams in Dayton, Ohio, and First Four Out are No. 1 seeds in the NIT—holds true. The public also understands that a 64-team bracket has four teams on each seed line.

In the very beginning, we actually used the terms "Last Four In" and "Last Four Out." I liked the way it sounded. But a former ESPN producer, Marc Carman, now at the Big Ten Network, correctly said, "It's really not the Last Four Out, it's the First Four Out." So about 10 or 12 years ago, we changed it. Regardless, the terms help synthesize the most important information for media and fans: who are the teams we should be focusing on? Every few years a team from my Next Four Out list gets a bid, so that grouping deserves some attention, but I can only remember one or two instances when a team got in that wasn't on either list or came out of the blue (at least to me).

Since the advent of the First Four in 2011, we now know the actual "Last Four In." There is no more guessing. In the old days, we could sort of guess based on seeding. They were the lowest-seeded at-large teams before teams from the so-called one-bid leagues appeared on the bracket. The final at-large teams could almost always be found among the No. 11 or No. 12 seeds. Yet because the voting for seeding is separate from that for selection, there wasn't necessarily a one-to-one correlation. That's no longer true. If your team is in Dayton—even the Dayton Flyers, as was the case in 2015—we know it was one of the last four to make the field.

As for the "First Four Out," somebody walks down the hall to the NIT committee—or jumps on their conference call—to tell them who their four top seeds will be. It's a seamless process now that the NCAA owns the NIT. It's also important for schools to know exactly where they stood in preparing for future seasons.

Two years ago the first team out was UNC-Greensboro. I had them among my "First Four Out" (team No. 70, to be precise). It was team No. 69 in actuality and got knocked out of the NCAA Tournament field when Oregon won the Pac-12 title game late Saturday night. If I'm affiliated with the Southern Conference, a league which these days might get an at-large bid once every 30 years, I would want to know that one of my teams was right there. What did UNCG do so that we can try to replicate it in the future? And if I'm the athletic director, I'm giving the head coach a bonus. What he did to earn a No. 1 seed in the NIT is just as hard—if not harder—for a Southern Conference team than a major conference member earning an NCAA bid. Think about it. There are far more middle-of-the-pack ACC or SEC teams in the NCAA Tournament than low-majors at the top of the NIT bracket. It's incredibly hard for those schools to make the NCAAs and nearly as hard to just miss.

So I'll take full credit for Last Four/First Four, which is just a way of simplifying the conversation. And I'm not going to lie: if I put four teams up on a screen, it generates a certain amount of interest. If I put eight teams on a screen, we just doubled the number of fanbases that consider that to be essential information.

The more recent concept of "Last Four Byes" can be a bit more confusing. A lot of people still don't understand what that means. Think of it this way: of the 36 at-large teams, 32 get a bye into the main bracket; the other four have to play in the First Four (officially the opening round). They've messed around with the terminology over the years. For a short time, they called the Dayton games the *first round*, meaning 60 teams were in the second round without playing or winning a game. Thankfully, this was changed pretty quickly.

It's significant to be in the First Four from a financial perspective. Occasionally schools call late in the season wanting to know their chances of going to Dayton. They want to go because it gives them a chance at another revenue unit. This is especially valuable for the four No. 16 seeds at the First Four. UMBC notwithstanding, the 16-seeds in the main bracket ain't winning. But the four in Dayton have a 50/50 shot at a second game—and a second unit. If you're running the Southwestern Athletic Conference or one of the other really low-major leagues, you can double your take by winning a First Four game. There's a pretty big difference between $1.7 million and $3.4 million. As the low-major conference commissioner told me once, "That's a lot of paper clips."

It's the same for the last four at-large teams. If you can go to Dayton and know you have a real chance to win, you can double your take in a 50/50 game. Otherwise you're a double-digit seed trying to beat a No. 5 or No. 6 seed. Even with all the legendary 5/12 upsets, the 12 seeds still win only 35 percent of the time in the round of 64. And that's not counting the momentum gained from winning a game while your opponent is idle.

In the First Four's first year of existence in 2011, Virginia Commonwealth went from the First Four to the Final Four and completely legitimized that element of the tournament. The trip to Dayton wasn't a consolation prize. It was a legitimate method of advancement in the competition. I didn't have VCU in the field that year. The Rams were among my First Four Out, and I was wrong eight ways to Sunday. VCU coach Shaka Smart (now at Texas) said he hoped I would never put one of his teams in the tournament because they reach the Final Four when I don't. Very funny. I would argue to this day that the Rams shouldn't have made the 2011 field, and Jerry Palm and I would have a death match about this. He still says VCU was obviously in. I would argue that being one of the last four at-large selections by definition means the Rams weren't obviously in or out. I would further argue that they may not have been the next best selection from their own league. But to VCU's credit, when given the opportunity, the Rams got hot and played their tails off.

All of which misses the larger and more essential point that we don't select enough good mid-major teams over the so-called "middling" majors—yes, my term. If VCU didn't make the field in 2011, if that committee took, say, Nebraska from a Power Five conference, we would have missed out on a magical run. That's why we need the Lunardi Rule: no teams with losing conference records and more opportunities for the VCUs of the world.

Another term associated with Bracketology that I'll happily take credit for is "body of work." Coaches, athletic directors, media, and fans always ask the same question: what's the one thing the committee looks for? The answer then and now is simple: there isn't any one thing. Even in the years in which RPI and schedule strength were the most significant elements, the committee still evaluated a team's full season. The term itself—body of work—is probably more academic than athletic. Ever been to Parent/Teacher Night as a parent? Your child gets a grade in a class from her or his total work in that class—not just the final exam, the group project, a book report, class participation, quizzes, or whatever. *Everything* factors into the grade. While the father might say, "My Suzie just got an A on her last seventh-grade social studies test," the teacher responds, "But Mr. Lunardi, Suzie's grade is on her body of work for the whole quarter."

Another term is "Who did you play and who did you beat?" I think I get credit for this, too. It's similar to taking a term like body of work and putting it into a true basketball context. As RPI and strength of schedule diminished in importance, we got a lot more committee talk about wins against Top 50 opponents. Teams needed to be able to point to victories over others in the field.

"Who did you play" is a question of scheduling, and "who did you beat" is a question of performance. I often add "where was the game" as a way of distinguishing teams that may have loaded up on home cooking.

There was a season in which Missouri coach Norm Stewart and his Tigers were in the conversation all the way through. But they didn't have any road wins, and Stewart, to his credit, knew it. In 2019–20 resurgent Rutgers had only one road win—at woeful Nebraska—before a final weekend triumph at Purdue punched the Scarlet Knights' would-be ticket. We were right to question the Knights, who despite several high-quality wins at home, weren't going to play any tournament games in Piscataway, New Jersey. Ultimately, Rutgers' home wins were so good that an NCAA bid was coming regardless. But we had to at least ask those questions. The where matters. Was it in Maui or on another neutral floor with a national TV audience? Or was it one of a dozen straight home games to make sure a team doesn't leave campus until the start of league play?

I used to give out the Rand McNally Award to the team or coach that went the longest into a season without playing a true road game. Almost every year somebody was able to eat only home cooking into January. Without mentioning individuals, it's probably coincidence that a coach named Boeheim and another named Krzyzewski were multiple winners. These are just facts. There are many years, when short of the old ACC/Big East Challenge or the current ACC/Big Ten Challenge, Syracuse, Duke, and others don't play *any* road games out of conference. They might play neutral-site games. They might go to the Virgin Islands, but they aren't going to someone else's gym. These guys didn't become Hall of Famers by being dumb. They know that road teams lose more than 70 percent of the time. If you play 10 home games in November and December, your average record as a Division I men's basketball team is going to be 7–3. If you play 10 road games instead, you're going to be 3–7 on average. I'm guessing most coaches would prefer to be 7–3. That's why in 2005 the RPI was finally weighted to increase the value of road and neutral games.

A term related to all of this is "Bracket Buster." This was an ESPN concoction, a programming tool to pair up teams from non-power conferences for a bit of late-season exposure. Tom Odjakjian and his former basketball programming team get the credit for this concept. The core of Bracket Buster involved selecting the best mid-major teams for a great slate of interconference games toward the end of the regular season. In addition to the best of the matchups airing on the ESPN networks, there was the all-important matter of resume boosting. And it worked. In 2006 George Mason's win at Wichita State in Bracket Busters helped propel the Patriots to an at-large bid and ultimately the Final Four. Along the way GMU even won a rematch with the Shockers in the Sweet 16.

At one time Bracket Busters also included the likes of Gonzaga, San Diego State, Creighton, and Davidson. It was a truly unique concept. Conference realignment along with year-over-year scheduling logistics led to its downfall. But it was fun while it lasted. It was also cool to be involved in the pairings. In its latter years, Andy Katz and I hosted a Bracket Busters Selection Show from the ESPNU studios in Charlotte. I would head south the day before and recommend the best matchups based on that season's Bracketology. The show aired about three weeks before the actual games, allowing for travel planning and marketing by the respective schools. The only thing teams knew in advance was whether or not they'd be a home or away participant that season.

It was fun to interview coaches and players and hear answers such as, "We're really excited to go to Omaha for Bracket Busters." No offense, but the next person excited about a trip to Omaha at the end of February will be the first. Yet in 2007 Drexel won its Bracket Busters game at Creighton and should have received an at-large bid. The Dragons also won at Syracuse, Villanova, and Temple that season. But it's a good thing the committee took Arkansas and its 7–9 SEC record because Drexel would have had a hard time duplicating the Razorbacks' blowout NCAA loss to Southern California. But I digress...

Eventually, the likes of Creighton and Butler became major conference teams through realignment. Gonzaga felt it had risen above the level of "Bracket Busters," which was certainly true. The Atlantic 10 never participated. Others bailed and frankly the number of at-large bids going to "Bracket Buster"-type teams was shrinking. What the game really needs is a reformed "Bracket Busters," a challenge between the middling majors and the top mid-majors with half of them being played on the mid-majors' courts. But we all know I have a better shot at being president of the United States than a true "Bracket Buster" of that type ever taking place. The chance that a power conference bubble team—let's say Minnesota—is going to play at Stephen F. Austin, well, it's not going to happen.

The way to do it would be to expand the NCAA Tournament and mandate these games. Imagine additional games on the two nights of the current First Four. These would be actual Bracket Buster games or neutral-court contests between the true bubble teams that season.

It would be appointment television, kind of like the ACC/Big Ten challenge but on a national scale. Now I love the conference challenges, and many of the games are important. But if you asked me who won the ACC/Big

Ten challenge in a given year, I'd have no idea. But if those matchups were part of the NCAA Tournament, they'd all know if it was the mid-major or majors. We'd be able to name the teams, the games, and where we were when we watched, say, UNC Greensboro beat Indiana to reach the field of 64. Such a format would change Bracketology a lot, but I'm willing to sacrifice it for the greater good—as long as I get to go to the games.

This perfectly transitions to one of Bracketology's greatest terms: the "bid stealer." In 2019 Buffalo was 32–4 with wins at West Virginia and Syracuse and a NET ranking of 15. The Bulls were going to the NCAA Tournament no matter what happened at the Mid-American Conference tournament. It turns out the Bulls won the MAC's automatic bid that year, but we can be sure there was a long list of bubble teams around the country pulling for them just the same. If Buffalo had stumbled, another MAC team would have captured the league's automatic qualifier, and the Bulls would have bumped another team (likely St. John's) from the at-large field.

This is the most common type of bid stealer: the unexpected mid-major AQ. A less frequent type comes out of the major conferences when a team goes on a run of big-time wins to salvage an automatic bid after an otherwise poor season. My favorite example was Georgia in the 2008

A Language All Its Own

SEC Tournament. Not only did the Bulldogs overcome a last-place finish in the SEC East, they also won four games in three days to take the tournament championship. *Four games in three days?* Yes, a tornado ripped through Atlanta on the Friday of the SEC Tournament, postponing Georgia's quarterfinal game against Kentucky. While the Georgia Dome was being repaired, the Bulldogs and Wildcats played Saturday morning at Georgia Tech, and the Bulldogs won in overtime. That night Georgia made it back to the Georgia Dome and took out Mississippi State before completing its miracle on Sunday with a title game win against Arkansas. The entire country was pulling for the Bulldogs—except for fans of the bubble team they pushed to the NIT. Georgia entered the NCAA Tournament with the lowest seed ever awarded (No. 14) to a major conference team. Then again, the Bulldogs were 13–16 (4–12 in conference) in the regular season. It was an accurate evaluation. Perhaps the committee learned a lesson from 2006, when Syracuse (19–11, 7–9 Big East) won four games in four days to salvage an NCAA bid. The Orange got a No. 5 seed for that run but ran out of gas against No. 12 Texas Tech in its NCAA opener.

Things really get crazy if there's a potential bid stealer playing on Selection Sunday itself. This requires the committee to have an either/or scenario in place. Let's say the Big Ten Championship Game tips at 3:45 PM eastern time

173

and features Michigan State against underdog Northwestern. There has to be a plan in case Northwestern wins. That contingency bracket has to be in the hands of CBS for the Selection Show at 6:00 PM eastern. It is the ultimate zero-sum game.

Of course, we monitor all scenarios from the infamous "Bracket Bunker," a term which originated long before it became a television staple. It dates back to my *Blue Ribbon* days when our tournament preview edition was produced out of the university communications office at St. Joe's. It was the infancy of Bracketology, and the bunker was real. No cameras, no satellite hits, just a half-dozen guys and a couple extra TVs. I kicked my SJU staff out of the office on Friday afternoon so the bracket crew could come in. We'd then work around the clock until Sunday night, surviving on unhealthy provisions and adrenaline.

The annual Sunday morning coffee visit from athletic director Don DiJulia was as welcome as a visit from Santa Claus. "I was fascinated by all the work they did in such a short weekend," the semi-retired DiJulia said. "I would stop by and offer encouragement. And I wanted to talk to Joe out of my own curiosity. I might say, 'I have Alabama as my last team in. What do you have?' When he started to put together his own formula, he was way above my pay grade. I would base it on who I'd seen and what their record was. I wasn't into any analytical approach. Joe put his field together based on the criteria that the NCAA was laying out there. He could speak to why Alabama was not getting in. He would tell me they lost five conference road games in a row, and in three of them they were favored. I didn't follow it that closely. That's where him being so sharp really took it to a whole new dimension."

As usual, DiJulia is being incredibly modest. He was the first person to ever share the NCAA principles and procedures with me. He was the first person to ever take me through a mock selection exercise. He opened more doors for me than exist at the Vatican. That his current SJU office is in the same building as the original Bracket Bunker is only fitting. Regis Annex never had it so good.

The last bit of Bracketology language is personal, and that's my on-air nickname: Joey Brackets. When Josh Elliott was in his first role at ESPN doing ESPNews segments, he came up with the name. When Elliott moved up to *SportsCenter*, so did "Joey Brackets." Heck, he once got to call me Joey Brackets on *Good Morning America*. One of the coolest things, and it's usually right around Championship Week, is when I walk into a conference tournament, and there are fans from multiple schools. People will start yelling out, "Joey Brackets!" I will admit to some vanity when that happens. I'll sign autographs as Joey Brackets and pose for pictures. Why not? I know in a few days it'll all be over and I'll be back to being Average Joe for another 51 weeks.

At the ESPN bunker in Bristol, Connecticut, more than a few of the college basketball producers shorten the nickname and just call me "Brackets." They'll throw it to me, and in my earpiece, I'll hear, "Brackets, what'cha got?" I just perk up. In a way everything I do is to ensure I'm ready at any point of the year—in season or out of season—to answer that question: "Brackets, what'cha got?"

CHAPTER EIGHT

Joey Brackets

People who don't know me but know what I do probably imagine that I'm a former college basketball coach or player. They probably think I'm about 6'1" with a soft touch from the outside and the ability to put it on the floor and drive to the hoop. Not so much.

My first exposure to basketball would have been like a lot of kids. There was a hoop and backboard my dad put up in the driveway attached to the garage. I had two brothers, Henry and Richard, who were considerably older. Henry is 15 years older, and Rich was seven years older. I was maybe seven or eight at the time. I was the runt of the litter in every way. When that hoop went up, Henry was finishing college, and Rich was entering high school. They would have games going on in the driveway with their friends. Like any admiring little brother, I wanted to at least watch the games—if not play. They humored me. I remember the ball; it was a Spalding. It was not one of those driveway balls with the big dimples. It felt soft in your hands. It was smooth but with a perfect grip. I remember always wanting to shoot with that one. Lord knows where that ball is today.

If you grew up in the Philadelphia area at that time in the '60s and '70s, college basketball was a big deal. The college doubleheaders played at the Palestra were televised on Channel 17 and usually on Wednesday and Saturday nights. Because Henry was in college at St. Joe's and played in the pep band, we watched the games from home. That's my first memory of watching college basketball—in black and white. All the Philly schools were playing big-time, non-league opponents. I watched Notre Dame, North Carolina, Syracuse, St. John's, and Georgetown come in to play the local schools. We also, of course, watched the games in the City Series when the locals played each other. That was titanic. That was the golden age of the Big 5 of La Salle, Penn, Saint Joseph's, Temple, and Villanova.

My brother brought home the game programs, and I studied them. I studied the stats, the names on the rosters, their high schools, and their hometowns. I tried to predict who would win strictly based on which teams were taller. If a team had two seven-footers, how could the other team possibly win? At that age the term *stiff* had not yet come into my vocabulary. Now, I say: "Give me a good 6'7" guy who can run, jump, dunk, and shoot over the 7' benchwarmer every time." Back then, I didn't know any better.

But I never played on an organized team in basketball. I played Little League baseball and a lot of hockey, wearing a Bobby Clarke jersey that almost still fits. But you have to understand: I was *really* little. I was no more going to get picked for a basketball team than I was going to be nominated for Surgeon General. I went to Catholic grade school. I'm sure it happens in public school, too, but in Catholic school, they always lined us up for the class picture by height. The smallest kid sat in the front row, in the center, and held up a little sign with the room number. I hold the school record because I did it eight straight years. I wasn't just the smallest boy in the class. I was the smallest *person* for eight straight years. Like Tony Dorsett and the first 99-yard touchdown run in the NFL, somebody might tie my record, but nobody is going to break it.

Height—or lack of it—wasn't the only reason I wasn't a serious basketball player. I could run fast but didn't have any signature basketball skills. I remember through high school and college occasionally playing pick-up basketball, but I'm not one of those gym rats who at 40, 50, or 60 years old was still in a rec league playing every Sunday night at the middle school gym. I've never been that person. So I had to get my fix in other ways. I remember at one point either late in college or right after college being asked, "What do you want to be?" Jokingly, I said I would love to be the "Bill James of college basketball." I had discovered *The Bill James Historical Baseball Abstract* series and was fascinated by it.

He's also a great writer. Because James is a stats guy, most people think that his books are going to be dryer than dry. Not so. His writing is phenomenal in every way as far back as you can get your hands on it. More significantly, I thought his differing approaches to baseball were a real breakthrough. I go back to some of those early '80s books. Sitting in my home office, I can look at a couple of them up on the shelf. So applying differing approaches to basketball seemed to fit.

My first exposure to basketball stats came from those St. Joe's game programs and also the 1966–67 NBA champion Philadelphia 76ers, whose 68–13 record was the best in league history at the time. I was in the first grade, but I remember their starting five even better than the alphabet: center Wilt Chamberlain, forward Luke Jackson, forward Chet Walker, guard Hal Greer, and guard Wali Jones. Chamberlain and Jones were from Overbrook High School right where I grew up, and Jones went to Villanova. The sixth man was Billy Cunningham, and their No. 1 draft pick was a rookie from Saint Joseph's named Matty Guokas. And the general manager happened to be Dr. Jack Ramsay, who had just finished a legendary coaching stint at St. Joe's.

So here I was in first grade, and so many parts of my world were already coming together. We can't find it, but my dad had a little black-and-white picture of me typing a Sixers' box score on his manual typewriter. Why was I doing that? God only knows. But it was a precursor to the kind of stuff I would one day do professionally.

For Christmas that year, I asked for a clock radio with a sleep timer on it. You could go to sleep with the radio on, and it would shut off when the timer ran out. Oh, the technology! Since I always wanted to stay up and listen to the 76ers games, this was a compromise with my mom. I'd fall asleep—maybe—listening to the games. I listened mostly because of Chamberlain. I was fascinated by his name, his height, his everything. Living in the Overbrook section of Philadelphia where he went to Overbrook High, I thought everybody got to grow up and root for their hometown hero. Didn't everybody have a favorite player from their neighborhood? I didn't know any better. Our home, Overbook High, and St. Joe's were in a three-mile radius. The Hawks were the preseason No. 1 team in *Sports Illustrated* in 1965–66, and the 1966–67 Sixers were once voted the greatest team in NBA history. Good times.

Obviously, the Boston Celtics were dominant overall. They had won eight straight titles before the 76ers won it all in 1967. It was a once-in-lifetime team. They beat the Cincinnati Royals, whose star was Oscar Robertson, in a best-of-five and then knocked off the Celtics in five games to win the East. Then they played the San Francisco Warriors. They had a chance to close out the series in five at home but lost and had to win Game Six on the road. I don't remember if it was on television. I only remember listening to the game from a place called the "Cow Palace."

Six years later the Sixers went from winning the most games in the league to going 9–73, the worst record in NBA history. Chamberlain had become a malcontent and was traded to the Los Angeles Lakers. The Sixers became a laughingstock in pretty short order. They rebounded from that with the great Dr. J teams and got to the finals in 1976–77, losing to the Portland Trail Blazers and Coach Ramsay.

My interest in basketball built gradually, but it wasn't my favorite sport growing up. Hockey was. My brothers played hockey. So I followed. My oldest brother was an original season-ticket holder of the expansion Philadelphia Flyers. The Flyers were born the year after the Sixers had their epic season. As the Sixers were descending, the Flyers were ascending. I still followed college basketball because of the Big 5. I remember Lew Alcindor and the Walton years of the UCLA dynasty. In 1971 Villanova went all the way to the NCAA championship game and lost to UCLA in the Astrodome. Howard Porter was their star. I watched that game on a neighbor's color TV because we didn't have one yet. Villanova made it to the Final Four over another Big 5 team, the University of Pennsylvania. The Quakers were undefeated and had beaten Villanova during the regular season on their way to the Big 5 title. But in the regional final far from the Palestra in Raleigh, North Carolina, Villanova hammered the Quakers 90–47. It remains one of the most shocking scores in college basketball history.

That 1971 NCAA Tournament is the first one I remember following. I was 10 years old. I was following it because there was a local school that went in undefeated, and another was expected to do well. There wasn't seeding back then, but if there had been, Penn would have been a No. 1 seed for sure. St. Joe's was also in that tournament, facing Villanova at the Palestra in the opening round. The Wildcats won, and the rest is history.

* * *

The first time I ever remember drawing a bracket I was sitting on the floor of the living room in the early 1970s with a piece of loose-leaf paper and penning a bracket with four names on it. Those names were Penn, Marquette, Houston, and UCLA, and they came out of the latest wire service polls in the newspaper. The first time I remember paying attention to tournament selections was in 1981. I was a junior at Saint Joseph's and an editor of *The Hawk*, which was our college paper. St. Joe's had won what was then the

East Coast Conference, precursor of the Patriot League, and waited to see what would become of its automatic NCAA bid. For reasons that defy understanding, I was in the college library at the time (surely not for an academic purpose) when the pairings came out.

It's a vivid memory, and I remember looking at the draw sheet when it first came out. St. Joe's was a No. 9 seed slated for a Thursday night 8/9 game at the Mideast Regional in Dayton, Ohio. At that time there were 48 teams in the field. So the top four in each region got a bye. When I saw that the Hawks were in the 8/9 game, I immediately thought, *If we win, we're going to get to play a No. 1 seed. We could be that team to pull the big upset.* It turned out that No. 1 seed was DePaul. The Blue Demons were not only a top seed, but also the top-ranked team in the country. They were coached by the legendary Ray Meyer and were led by consensus National Player of the Year Mark Aguirre. After beating Creighton 59–57 in the 8/9 game, the Hawks were set to play DePaul on Saturday afternoon.

Truth be told, St. Joe's didn't belong on the court with DePaul. Aguirre and Terry Cummings would become NBA All-Stars, and the Blue Demons were No. 1 in the country for the second year in a row. UCLA had upset them in their first game of the 1980 NCAA Tournament. So there was no way the Demons would be anything but focused this time around. And my Hawks weren't the UCLA Bruins. But head coach Jim Lynam had perfected a four-to-score offense throughout the year. The Hawks slowed everything down, DePaul never pressed, and the score was in the 40s as the final minutes ticked away. When DePaul's Skip Dillard, an 84 percent free-throw shooter, missed the front end of a one-and-one in the final seconds, the Hawks went the length of the floor for a game-winning layup. The score—49–48— and scene galvanized both my love of the tournament and the possibilities in every bracket.

Earlier that week I had asked a girl named Pam Miller out for a date. I had to postpone it when the Hawks made the tournament and postpone again because of our subsequent trip to the Sweet 16. With the Final Four coming to the Spectrum in Philadelphia on the last weekend of the month, our first date wasn't happening anytime soon. Even though that first date didn't come until April 1 after the national championship game, she married me anyway. I blame it all on that 8/9 game in Dayton.

Meanwhile, in the Sweet 16, the Hawks nipped Boston College 42–41. They were in the Elite Eight, having won two of their three games by a single point and the other by two. The run came to a crashing halt in the Elite Eight on the campus of Indiana University, where the Hawks had to face the Hoosiers in Assembly Hall. Needless to say, the matchup against Isaiah Thomas & Co. was lopsided from the start. St. Joe's may have been one step away from a Final Four berth in Philadelphia, but it was at Indiana, and the Hoosiers would cut down the nets at the Spectrum just as they had during its undefeated season of 1976.

Nonetheless, I had gone from a 10 year old drawing up a bracket on loose-leaf paper in the living room to a 20 year old covering the NCAA Tournament and Final Four in his hometown. By the time I was 35 in the mid-1990s, I was doing brackets for a national audience on a fledgling website called ESPN Sports Zone. ESPN was outsourcing a website to get into the Internet business. And this was all from a guy who can't touch the rim without a ladder.

The first time I tracked Bracketology performance came in 1997, and I missed one team out of what was then a 64-team field. I put in Southwest Missouri State, and the team I left out was Southern California. To this day I've made more than a few mistakes picking the high-quality mid-major ahead of the middling major. I remember keeping my score that year because St. Joe's had won the Atlantic 10 and made the tournament as a No. 4 seed. It was the Hawks' first NCAA bid since 1986, and that was the longest gap in the history of the school. Because of that there was a selection watch party on campus.

I left the *Blue Ribbon* bunker—the original bunker, which was in my office on one side of campus—to run over to Alumni Memorial Fieldhouse to be with the team. Long after the Hawks had been announced in the field, head coach Phil Martelli kept looking at me as I wrote down every team as it came up on CBS. Don DiJulia asked, "How did you do?" When I finally compared the actual bracket to mine, I realized I missed one.

Others thought this was incredible, but I don't remember thinking of it as a big deal. If anything, I was probably more upset about Southwest Missouri State than the 63 I got right. Having been awake for 50 straight hours doing brackets and *Blue Ribbon*, I couldn't imagine anybody missing a team under those circumstances. Subconsciously, I'm sure I thought, *How dare they not use all of my picks?* It was only later that I found out how much I *didn't* know about the procedures, data, and metrics that went into the committee's final bracket. Back then it was probably an accident that I got 63 right, as opposed to today, when so many of us are replicating the process so closely that we should be right most of the time.

It's not normal to spend as much time as I do predicting the brackets just so the average fan can look to see where their team *might* be seeded. For most of America, of course, the bracket is something to fill out *after* the teams are announced and to predict how the games will turn out.

I'm often asked if I fill out a bracket and how good I am at that. Absolutely, I fill out a bracket (or two or three). After all, I'm a college basketball fan. After doing this for so many years, the public waits for my game picks with great anticipation, even though it's a broader public at that point. More casual observers don't understand that Bracketology is the science of picking the field, *not* picking the winners. I'm here to report with a gallon of truth serum that I'm no better at the latter than the secretary in your office, the guy at the end of the bar, your neighbor, or, in one memorable case, our own cocker spaniel.

In the 1998 tournament, our beloved cocker named Murray did quite well when, ahem, Murray State had a memorable run to the Sweet 16. In our family pool tracked on our favorite white board in the basement, Murray (the dog) had Murray State (the school) going far and also picked teams with dog nicknames against all the teams with cat nicknames. With neither a dog or a cat in the game, Murray always picked—wait for it—the *underdog*. And that's how a bracketologist lost to a cocker spaniel.

I've got to tell you those things happen to me more years than I want to admit. It used to irritate me because I thought of myself as a real expert. The notion that Bracketology conveyed a magic power to pick the winners was dispelled systematically over time. It was a humbling realization that the outcomes of these games were pretty darn random. The sooner I made peace with that, the more I was able to enjoy the tournament. By the 2000s when I started showing up at tournament venues more regularly as a fan, people started coming up to me at snack bars, sitting in the stands, or walking along press row. They call out happily, "I'm beating you." To which I can only respond, "Get in line."

I've lost to my mom, my daughters, my secretary, and a dog. It's become a rite of passage for me to spout off expertise all season long and then be humbled come tournament time. Clearly, my expertise ends the minute the ball goes up on Thursday afternoon. Plus, by that point I'm already working on *next year's* bracket. But I can't lie. I do peek at the "Beat the Bracketologist" group on the ESPN.com Tournament Challenge to see how I'm doing.

The person I want to beat the most is Mrs. Bracketology. Not because Pam is a college basketball expert—though she's been to more games than most—but because she likes to take credit for me being in this business. Not only is she there for me on an ongoing basis, but she also gave me a gigantic push right at the start. We were in the airport in October 1985 coming back from our honeymoon. That would be the time of year to buy all the preseason magazines. I made my annual purchase of *Street & Smith's* and other publications of the same ilk. I remember reading them on the plane and being, well, less than supportive of their collective wisdom. Now I have no ill will toward the editors of those publications or their writers and stringers. I fully understand they were going to press in the summer in order to hit the stands when practices began. They couldn't help but print old information. Still, as I was reading, Pam heard me muttering "this is wrong" or "that's dumb." She said, "If you think you're so much better, why don't you try writing for one of these publications?" As my dad liked to say, "Behind every successful man is a surprised woman."

Over the next year or so, we put a bunch of clips together and sent them out to all the preseason publications. The first to respond was the *Blue Ribbon*, and my first national assignment came shortly thereafter. Chris Wallace gave me the Ivy League for *Blue Ribbon*, and I went to town on it. The write-ups must have been okay, as Wallace gave me more assignments and eventually asked for help in editing the book and assigning other writers.

I don't know that happens without Pam's encouragement. Without it, I might still be a stringer for the *Delaware County Daily Times*. It was a strong suburban daily. Newspapers were still big enough and successful enough to pay a freelancer to cover college basketball part-time. There were alums from all the Philly area schools among its readership, and there were players from the local high schools starring for the college teams. It made sense. Those were really happy memories.

Those were also the clips I sent along to Wallace. Rollie Massimino was in those clips and so was John Chaney. The entire Big 5 and Drexel were in those clips, and I was covering NCAA Tournament games on an annual basis. I look back now and realize how fortunate I was to have had that kind of proving ground. I was a pretty good writer and could be really good on deadline. There's value in that. Sometimes out-of-town papers would hire me if a team came into Philly and they weren't sending a beat guy. That happened not just in basketball; it happened with the Philadelphia Phillies, Flyers, and 76ers. I got a lot of work that way. At that time the stars in sports media were the beat writers, not the talking heads on TV. We made fun of them. They were the Ken dolls, and we were the smart ones. Little did I know that I would one day become a miniature Ken doll. I'm now one of the people that I probably would have made fun of 30 years ago.

Pam supported every step of the journey. We were married in 1985, and our first daughter, Emily, was born in 1994. Without a little one at home for so many years, I was out chasing sportswriting assignments in addition to my regular job. The extra income was certainly welcome, but it wasn't changing our tax bracket. I did it because I loved doing it.

It's also fair to say Pam has a way of keeping me humble. After David Smale and I first discussed this book, I went home and told her there was an accomplished author in Kansas City who wanted to do a book with me. She said rather incredulously, "About you?" I said, "No, the evolution of Bracketology" and I showed her the great Bracketology article he wrote for the 2019 Final Four program. There have been articles like that done pretty much every year for a decade or more. She said, "Are you sure that's a book? It sounds more like a pamphlet."

Smale wasn't the first to approach me about a book, but he came at the right time and was far and away the most persistent. I was already transitioning in my professional life and had more time to pursue these kinds of things. When you have a following of 240,000 people on Twitter, you start to think maybe there is a market for more than a pamphlet.

* * *

I have mentioned Dick Vitale and his so-called schtick. If I'm being honest, I see a little bit of that in me. I go against the norm. He's a bald, glass-eyed Italian from Jersey. I'm the midget bracketologist from Philly who couldn't play a lick, and we're both thrilled to be involved in our favorite sport. There was a producer in my early days on ESPNews who always called me "Smiling Joe." He always asked why I was always smiling. "I could have a real job," I said. "I'm so happy doing this instead!"

I tend to be self-deprecating, but I also have a healthy ego. Yet I'd like to think I know my place. I grew up in a house with two bright parents and two very smart older brothers. When you're the little one, you get smacked down pretty good. And our family certainly kept me humble over the years. At the same time, I know they're proud. We lost Rich to pancreatic cancer in 2013, and that was awful. But when I hear myself get "too big for my britches," as my mom used to say, I hear Rich over my shoulder as a reminder of what's really important. And Henry, now 75 and a full-time grandfather, is certainly no wallflower when offering an opinion is required. Back when I was mostly doing St. Joe's games behind the dial, my dad always said I had a face for radio. He was gone before most of the TV stuff happened. But I guarantee from wherever he's watching, he's saying, "I can't believe they're paying him to talk because his mother and I would have paid double to have him shut up."

I close my eyes and hear these voices. It's not negative motivation like bulletin-board material. Instead it feels very loving. To know how supported I was and how proud they would be is something to cherish as I hit 60 years old. No matter what age you are, you want to make your parents proud. If in some goofy, unimportant way, I'm making people proud through Bracketology, so be it.

I also have a very intelligent and loving spouse, who has a doctorate in psychology and a profession of her own. We have two extremely bright daughters. Both of them are college graduates and are pursuing worthwhile lives of their own. Just because I occasionally get written about doesn't make me all that. Even if I have become the "Bill James of college basketball" as I hoped, I'm probably the fourth smartest person in the house (and maybe the fifth during those periods of time when we have a dog). I know Murray believes that, as well as his successors, Tucker and Sam.

Our daughters, Emily and Lizzy, who is four years younger, both liked to send me pictures from college. Picture your own daughter at a frat party surrounded by a group that just discovered she's related to the "bracket guy." I would certainly never hold that over anyone who came into contact with either of my lovely daughters or threaten said individuals in any way with my fame or status. Just don't look askance at one of my girls.

All kidding aside, handling criticism is part of the job. I can't tell you how many times I've heard someone say, "I'd love to trade jobs with Joe Lunardi. All I have to do is watch basketball and pick who I think will be selected." That'd be like me saying, "It would be nice to be a college football coach because you only have to work Saturdays." Or: "It would be nice to be a pastor because you only have to work Sundays."

Handling criticism usually depends on what my level of sleep deprivation is at the time. Mostly it rolls off my back, but I'm human just like the committee members. I prefer praise to criticism, which seems pretty fundamental to human nature. But does it get under my skin sometimes? Absolutely, depending on the source. If it's someone I respect or have a relationship with, it might cut deeper than someone hiding behind an anonymous screen name on social media. The latter can be downright comical.

In 2004, the year Saint Joseph's finished the regular season undefeated, most forecasters had the Hawks as a No. 1 seed by mid-January. I took an extra week or two to elevate them, fearing the inevitable cries of homerism. Instead, the criticism came a little closer to home. One Friday afternoon during a weekly chat on ESPN.com, I got a bunch of questions from around the country, including from Philadelphia and the St. Joe's campus. I remember one in particular. The guy started out questioning my heritage and manhood and then went after my knowledge of college basketball. He turned out to be an SJU student. He wrote, "I'll bet you've never heard of St. Joe's or Jameer Nelson, our star player. You only like Duke and Kentucky and the big-name teams."

Maybe I should have ignored it, but I posted what I thought was an appropriate reply. "I know about St. Joe's. I'm a 1982 graduate, have worked on campus for 20 years, and am sitting in an office probably about 300 yards from your dorm room. Let's meet in front of the library in 15 minutes."

As I've said many times, you can take your work seriously without taking yourself too seriously. I try to let it roll off my back, but we're all human. For an hour or two near the end of the aborted 2020 season, Indiana coach Archie Miller was a complete jackass. His public comments toward me were out of line. That said, I can't imagine the amount of pressure the head coach of the Hoosiers is under to make the NCAA Tournament. I was pretty upset when I saw the clip, if only because Miller and I have a friendly relationship. But I wasn't going on television to make it worse just because a guy had a bad day at the office. Sometimes I have a bad day at the office too. But at the end of the day, we're arguing over whether a basketball team's record is good enough for an at-large bid. Nobody died. Most of us don't have to do a press conference when something goes wrong at work. I don't think Miller's tantrum makes him a fundamentally bad person or me a fundamentally good person.

I believe wholeheartedly that sometimes you laugh to keep from crying. A sense of humor is an indispensable life tool, and it's *really* indispensable in Bracketology. My dad liked to say, "Life is too serious to be taken seriously." I can hear that as if he just walked in the door.

I don't laugh when I miss teams on Selection Sunday, at least not initially. I usually start by thinking the committee was wrong, that they didn't know what they were doing. I'll recover eventually and most of the time be able to say to myself, *I can see what they were thinking.* Most of the time. There are times when the committee just flat-out misses a call, like a referee. There are times I flat-out miss a call, like another referee. Most of the time—the *vast* majority of the time—we're talking about shades of gray. That's when you have to laugh it off, take your medicine with good humor, and maybe make fun of yourself for not being perfect.

I once went to a charity function in Philadelphia and heard former major leaguer Rex Hudler, now a broadcaster, say, "There are two kinds of people in the world: drains and fountains. It's up to you." I really believe that. Bracketology allows me to be a fountain most of the time. That's pretty darned good, and I try to share that joy. It'll be time to stop if I ever get jaded. I'm getting paid to watch games and talk about them. That's as good as it gets.

BRACKETOLOGY

* * *

In January of 2017, I was in Dayton, Ohio, as the sideline reporter for a Friday night ESPN2 game between Dayton and George Washington. It was the start of major conference play across the country, and my job was to help tee up the next two months for our viewers. Adam Amin did the play-by-play, and the color man was Craig Robinson, the former Brown and Oregon State coach. Currently executive director of the NABC, Robinson is also Michelle Obama's brother. As it happened, we were in the last weeks of President Obama's second term. I didn't know Robinson that well, but during a production meeting, I said, "I have kind of a non-basketball question." He looked at me and smiled, "Yes, the big guy knows who you are."

Man, was I jacked. For years ESPN put President Obama's bracket on the screen next to mine. It was Bracket-ology versus Barack-etology. He was tough to beat. He watched games and knew the teams and he wisely went with a lot of chalk.

In May of 2017, my father-in-law, Ted Miller, arranged a group golf trip to Ireland. He had gotten me to take golf seriously years before because, as another proud father of two daughters, he looked at me as the "son he never had." He'd been bugging me for years to take an overseas golf trip, so I was one of 10 who lost a ball or two along the Irish coast. On the last day of the trip, we were playing a truly outrageous course, Old Head, on the south coast of Ireland. If this was your last day on Earth, Old Head would be an okay spot to spend it. I was having a pretty good day. We got to a par-5, and, shockingly, I hit a big-time slice that got caught up in the wind. The shot went a full two holes right to a hole we'd played about 45 minutes before. Old Head is a bucket list course. You've got to win a pseudo-lottery just to get a tee time. So I didn't want to be that guy who held up the entire place. I assumed at least one other group was ready to scream at me, so I was about to pick up my ball and run back. Instead, as I bent to grab the ball, someone in the group I was interrupting yelled out, "Joey Brackets, don't worry about it. Just move Florida up."

All of a sudden, a guy with a Florida hat starts doing the Gator Chomp. In Kinsale, Ireland, of all places. And, yes, an adult beverage or two were consumed after the round, during which I drove a downhill par-4 for a birdie.

Particularly in the age of social media, people will draw conclusions about you based on little or no facts. They'll post things like: "He's stuck on himself," "He's an egomaniac," "He hates my school," "He hates our league," or "He thinks he's a know-it-all." (Author's note: only that last one is true.)

We all make comments about people we don't know mostly because there are no repercussions.

A bigger pitfall during the season is not having any down time. I get "urgent" phone calls nonstop. Working for a 24/7 sports-and news-gathering organization, it's only natural for the powers-that-be to want my information in a timely fashion. But it's not just the people signing my paycheck. There are times I feel everyone in college basketball thinks they have a right to know what I'm thinking as soon as I'm thinking it. That's when I have to set some limits around who gets what information and when. The latest bubble teams belong on ESPN wraps, not a local radio show or a random Twitter account. My assumption has always been that there is no such thing as inside information. It's only a matter of time before anything becomes outside information. Part of my job has become prioritizing information correctly. At peak times my priorities have to be (in order): ESPN, ESPN.com, the college basketball news desk, etc. Whenever I can, I'll take time for beat reporters, local radio stations, student media, and even general social media.

But there are only so many hours in a day, and there is a period of time from the Super Bowl until Selection Sunday during which there are more demands of me than there are hours in a day—at least the waking hours in a day. I have to triage. That means I'm saying no to some people and I'm sure that some take that as me big-timing them or being a jerk. For the record I'm not intentionally big-timing anyone. If I'm a jerk, it's because I already was one.

After the aborted 2019–20 season, I did an interview for a small daily in upstate New York. The writer was pursuing the story of a 14-year-old who had me on his podcast. He was a precocious middle-schooler trying to break into sports media in the time of quarantine, hoping to land some big fish as guests. I'm a medium fish at best, but I said yes. I was happy to do it and very much remember what that age was like. People helped me, too. It was different types of media at a different time, but helping is helping.

One year during Championship Week, I was in Bristol, Connecticut, doing my thing. I had a long enough break to go out and get something to eat one night. Most basketball evenings I can't do that. You get to the studio around 4:00 or 5:00 PM and work through dinner. Hopefully, there's time to grab something in the cafeteria. For whatever reason I had an hour or two on this occasion. I had time for a real meal with a vegetable. An Outback Steakhouse had just come to the next town over in Southington, Connecticut, and that qualified as high cuisine. I was having dinner at the bar, watching whatever games were on that night. A segment came on that we had taped earlier in the evening.

There I was on the screen, spouting off about whatever, and a guy, who I'd been talking to at the bar, was looking at the screen, looking at me, and looking back at the screen with a puzzled look on his face. I said, "That's my twin brother. We all think he's a jerk."

The man joined right in. "I don't like him either; he's never right." So I played along. Walking out of the restaurant, the man handed me his business card, and I did the same. He turned white. I said, "It's okay. Don't worry about it." Now that's funny.

CHAPTER NINE

Bracketology: The Insiders' Take

When claiming responsibility for something that has the attention of the nation's college basketball fans for several months each year, you know a whole bunch of people entrenched in the sport will have their opinions about your creation. One would hope the opinions are positive, but any attention is good attention. As actor George M. Cohan once said, "I don't care what they say about me as long as they spell my name right."

I wanted to get a cross-section of people involved in college basketball, including current or former coaches, administrators, journalists, and others throughout the country and find out their takes. Many hardly think I'm all that. So it's a good way to learn their unbiased thoughts on Bracketology.

What do you think of Bracketology?

"I probably bring a special perspective. Being at a small college for a while, I was a huge Bracketology guy. I know it's not legal for coaches to bet on the NCAA Tournament, and, of course, we don't, but back in my small college days, I may have won a couple of beers predicting games. And my source was Bracketology."

—*Chris Beard, Texas Tech head coach*

"Obviously, it's the No. 1 tool you use to try to figure out where you stand as far as the NCAA Tournament. It's not 100 percent, but nothing is. It's the one you look at first and it has been for a long time. As soon as you see yourself in the First Four Out, you have to be concerned. If you think you're in, you have to adjust. It has a lot of credibility. It's not foolproof, but it's the one that's the most easily available."

—*Randy Bennett, St. Mary's head coach*

"First of all, I think it's an unbelievable nickname: 'Joey Brackets.' When the whole thing got started, I thought it was a great thing for college basketball. I always thought he put us lower in his brackets because we were in Pittsburgh, and he is a Philly guy. But it's been unbelievable. [Bracketology] is great and it's helped college basketball. It fits on one sheet. You've got the brackets and the seeding. Anybody can figure out how to pick a team and advance them. You've even got the ability to cheat with the seeds. Anybody can be a part of the tournament because of the bracket. That's why those three weeks in March are the biggest sporting event in the country. The bracket is simple, concise, and easy to follow."

—*Jamie Dixon, TCU head coach, former Pitt head coach*

"It's tremendous for the game. Fans love it. They like to see where their team is. At the end of the day, everyone knows when Joe says something, it's usually right. From a coaching standpoint, I think it tells you where your team might be and the work you have to do to move up. Any exposure for college basketball is tremendous, and Joe has brought that with Bracketology."

—*Scott Drew, Baylor head coach*

"Bracketology has been great for promotion and interest in the tournament, in particular, but [also] the sport in general. It makes the connection between the tournament in March to even the preseason. It's an incredible promotional vehicle for one of the great sporting events in the world."

—*Dan Gavitt, NCAA men's basketball senior*
vice president and son of Big East founder Dave Gavitt

"It's a starting point. We live in a society where people want to feel like insiders. People want information. We have a tremendous fanbase, and because of that, people want to debate. By creating Bracketology, you're opening the conversation. It gives [fans] something to talk about. Are you in or out? It's really good for the sport, especially when some people think it's only relevant for one month. Bracketology is a 12-month sport. It opens up the conversation of who could be good—even in the summer months—and who is living up to their potential. During the season who has emerged? Who is struggling and who needs to win a big game? It makes each game more important. For ESPN that's probably the greatest value. It creates conversation."

—Seth Greenberg, ESPN college basketball analyst

"It's interesting for the fans. It gets the fans engaged. For [coaches] I don't think it makes all that much difference. You kind of know where you're going to be seeded."

—Bob Huggins, West Virginia head coach

"I was with Joe at the beginning when we were doing the *Blue Ribbon Yearbook*. It's a great phenomenon. I took it to a new level for eight years with the President [Obama] doing 'Baracketology.' That took on a life of its own. It's a great way to mainstream something in the American culture that everyone can relate to. A majority of people are an alum of somewhere. It's an event that touches more states than any professional league. You can have someone who doesn't care about the sport or one who is passionate about college basketball. They both can fill out a bracket and have a connection. That's something that has transcended into other aspects of our lives. As the tournament has gotten bigger, [Bracketology] has gotten bigger. The interest in it is bigger for all of us. It's transcended sports. It's something that's so easy to do. It's a fun way to compare and contrast anything from cereal to fast food restaurants."

—Andy Katz, FOX Sports and NCAA.com reporter

"It's become great entertainment year-round. Joe and others have gotten to be quite accurate. Fans love it. I know Joe puts a lot of time into it. Sometimes it can drive coaches and players crazy, but I think it's been great for the game."

—*Lon Kruger, Oklahoma head coach*

"As a fan I think it's great. I think most fans are fairly regional. They follow their team or teams in their area or conference. You might know the ACC standings, but you don't know the Pac-12 standings. More importantly, you don't know how a 20–10 record in the ACC compares to a 20–10 record in the Pac-12. Bracketology is a really good tool to help people talk and debate. As a coach I think Bracketology is very distracting and hard to convey to the players that it's just conjecture. If you're trying to get into the NCAA Tournament, no one sends you a list of criteria. They don't say, 'If you win 23 games, you're in,' or 'If you win eight road games, you're in.' It's just speculation. Now, it's really well-informed speculation. If we were to hold the bracketologists to what they say on January 10, they might not come out with [a new bracket] every day. They're predicting how the committee would vote if the season ended on that day. It's a unique idea, but through the season, it's a distraction and a little bit of a pain for a coach."

—*Chris Mooney, Richmond head coach*

"It promotes the tournament and keeps people involved. Joe Lunardi does a great job of doing his homework and presenting it to people. I've known Joe for a long time. I think he's a fabulous human, and he's done a fabulous job with Bracketology." [Author's note: Tom is fabulous, too, but he's not a very good judge of character.]

—*Tom O'Connor, former George Mason athletic director, 2008 Selection Committee chair*

"I love it. I'm a coach, but I'm a fan at heart. So I look at it all the time. If I look at the preseason field and see we're projected to play in Albany, I'm like, 'Let's go to Albany right now.' In my last year at Murray State, I was on Skype with his class at St. Joe's. He brought me in because I thought our team deserved to be in the tournament, but we didn't make it. There was a lot of debate. It's amazing that he can get it so close—give or take one or two teams. Being in [the Big 12] now is great because you have a chance to get a quality win every single night. You've got a chance to move the needle every single night. That's huge. Night in, night out, the competitiveness is off the charts. But there's still a part of me that likes to see two teams from the OVC get in because that's where I laid my foundation."

—*Steve Prohm, Iowa State head coach*

"Anything that is data-based, that makes the process more transparent, is valuable. Joe understood the RPI formula. There are people who looked at the RPI, but Joe knew it well enough that he could tell you why someone was rated where they were. He also knew there were outliers sometimes. The RPI wasn't a perfect system. There were obvious outliers every year, and Joe knew why there were. I think who makes the tournament, where they're seeded, and where they go are huge issues for the public. The more transparency we can have the better, and Joe certainly helped with that. I go back to when I was young. My grandpa was blind. He would tell us this poem called 'The Blind Men and the Elephant.' It starts: 'It was six men of Indostan, to learning much inclined, who went to see the Elephant [though all of them were blind], that each by observation might satisfy his mind.'

"Each of the six blind men grabbed a different part of the elephant. Though each one drew conclusions that were perfectly logical based on what they saw, those conclusions weren't very logical when they looked at the whole elephant. The poem ends, 'Though each was partly in the right, all were in the wrong,' because they didn't see the entire elephant. In this process of selecting teams, seeding teams, and sending them places, people draw all kinds of conclusions based on their level of information. What seems perfectly logical to them—we beat this team, and they're rated above us; we should be higher—they see a very small part of the elephant. Joe was one of the first people nationally to communicate and develop a system based on data. I think it was very valuable. I can't tell you how much the committee used it. I certainly looked at it. I don't know how much coaches and players look at it. I'm sure it is a discussion item. But I know it's huge to the fans. It helped educate the fans on the process."

—Bruce Rasmussen, Creighton athletic director, 2018 Selection Committee chair

"I have always admired those who have such knowledge about how the brackets will work out. It is a real art. Joe has been a true leader in the process of forecasting the field for March Madness."

—Sister Jean Dolores-Schmidt, Loyola Chicago chaplain

"I feel it's kind of like a preseason All-America team. It's something for everyone to talk about, but it doesn't mean much until February. Then it actually starts having meaning. I actually enjoy following it. I think it's better for fans than coaches. The one thing Joe has done is base his predictions on real information that is going to be thought about in the minds of the committee members. It's pretty real. I enjoy looking at it. But to get hung up on where you're seeded in December doesn't mean much."

—Bill Self, Kansas head coach

"Honestly, I don't put any thought into it."

—*Shaka Smart, Texas head coach*

"The in-depth coverage for the games is amazing. I don't think the guy sleeps at all. He has done a fantastic job of whetting the appetite of people. He creates a lot of debate and excitement. I love his enthusiasm for and interest in the game. I think it's very positive. I think Joe should be commended for his incredible effort and work ethic. His work ethic is off the charts."

—*Dick Vitale, ESPN college basketball analyst*

"Bracketology has become a big part of college basketball. The way it has evolved over the years has been amazing. Joe's been front and center through it all."

—*Steve Watson, Loyola Chicago athletic director*

"As an assistant coach, I watched it all the time. My assistants do now. But as a head coach, I try not to pay attention. It's like predictions. You've got to worry about what you can control on a daily basis. That's getting the guys ready and making the most of each day. It creates a lot of excitement for the fans. That's what they're looking for. The run to the Final Four is so much a part of our American culture. If it helps basketball, that's a great thing. Everybody is watching it. People who aren't really fans get involved. People fill out their brackets and they want to see who's in. It's a very important part of American culture and it's great for college basketball. It's really helped the game grow."

—*Bruce Weber, Kansas State head coach*

"Bracketology has become an art. It's added to the game and kept the interest of the general public. It continues to grow. Through the years you've seen Joe expand the number of offerings he's had related to Bracketology. I enjoy it. It's my 'cup of coffee' in the morning during the season. He's been so good through the years with his data. It's something that has to be paid attention to."

—*Aaron Woliczko, West Coast*
Conference administrator and
former University of the Pacific assistant coach

"Bracketology is a great marketing tool for the NCAA. As the season enters the home stretch of February and into March, it's an easy way for fans to get a handle on which teams are positioned to compete for the final at-large spots."

—*Jay Wright, Villanova head coach*

Have you ever used Bracketology as a way to motivate your players?

"Usually the players know it before I do. They've already been told or they checked it themselves. But when you know you're in that situation, it puts extra pressure on you. You have to go in with the mentality of controlling what you can control and not being overly nervous or uptight. But if Joe says you're Last Four In or First Four Out, that definitely spikes the sense of urgency. Bracketology does give you a true sense of where you are. Kids look at the mock drafts, and they're totally wrong. Joe isn't wrong."

—*Scott Drew, Baylor head coach*

"No, because every team has a bracketologist. We never shied away from the bubble conversation. We never said, 'We don't care about what people are saying.' Come February it's part of the conversation. You can't hide from it. You almost have to embrace it. It's not like the kids aren't going to know that if you beat Duke, it's a good win, or if you lose a home game, it's a bad loss. They understand it. Everyone's aware of it. There's someone on your team—whether it's your video guy, your operations guy, your manager, a walk-on—there's someone who is your team's bracketologist. That's the conversation they're having in the locker room. I embraced it. I didn't hold it over guys' heads because I didn't have to. They knew what was important. They knew the opportunities in front of them. If you beat a Top 10 team, that would turn heads. If you lose to a team from the bottom third of your conference, that's going to hurt you. I was very aware of it. I was the guy who, when we beat Duke in front of *College*

GameDay, and Vitale said, 'Put them in the Dance,' I said, 'There's a lot of basketball to play' because I understood how fragile it was. And we didn't get in that year."

—*Seth Greenberg, ESPN analyst*
and former Virginia Tech head coach

"We don't talk to our players about that because we want preparation to be the same for every game. But we know they're fans and we know they know. They talk about it among themselves. They're aware of what's going on."

—*Lon Kruger, Oklahoma head coach*

Some coaches aren't totally forthcoming. Shaka Smart, now the head coach at Texas, took some rightful jabs at me when his Virginia Commonwealth team reached the Final Four in 2011. VCU finished the regular season 28–12 and 12–6 in the Colonial Athletic Association but lost in the championship game of the conference tournament. I had them in my First Four Out, but they received a controversial (at the time) at-large bid. In the new First Four, the Rams defeated Southern California. They knocked off Georgetown and Purdue in the next two rounds to advance to the Sweet 16. There they defeated Florida State to advance to the Elite Eight, where they beat top-seeded Kansas to complete a truly remarkable run to the Final Four.

Smart quipped that he hoped I always had his squad in my First Four Out because it brought them good luck. When approached about that recently, Smart said, "I don't remember saying that, but if he says I did, I probably did. I don't put a whole lot of stock into it. It's done for the fans and it's exciting for them. For us it's about being in the moment. Bracketology is all about the future."

If you listen to talk radio, you've probably heard coaches say they never read the paper, listen to talk radio, or follow social media. If you believe that, I've got some oceanfront land in Montana to sell you. But some coaches are a little more upfront than others.

Do coaches pay more attention to Bracketology than they admit?

"If you're a team that's on the bubble, you look at it every day. I readily admit that it's something I look at, and once you do, it's in your head. Where you see your team's name, you know [the actual selections will be] pretty close to that. There are rarely times when someone comes from out of left field. He may be off, but he's not off by much. It's a valuable resource. It tells you where you stand."

—*Randy Bennett, St. Mary's head coach*

"Everyone pays attention. That's like the guys who say they don't read the newspaper. Everyone pays attention. They may not be consumed by it, but someone on that staff pays close attention to it. They know how many spots are available. After we'd get knocked out of the ACC Tournament, I knew who we were competing against for the last spots. Coaches can say what they want. There's a reason Joe gets phone calls. The misconception about Joe is that people think his brackets are his opinion about who should get in. It's his opinion about what the committee is going to do. That's a big difference. Joe is looking through the prism of the committee. He's got models, I'm sure. His model says, 'This team is one of the First Four Out.' His model is [only] related to that season's field."

—Seth Greenberg, ESPN analyst
and former Virginia Tech head coach

"It depends on where we are [relative to the bubble]. You have to give it some attention. It's a difficult task to compare a mid-major team with an outstanding record with a high-major team with a better-than-average record. Is it harder to have fewer wins, but two of those are against Indiana and Ohio State? Or is it harder to win 90 percent of your games? I think you have to pay attention to it to a certain degree. They've created this formula called NET, but then they'll tell you that it's only a guide. If the NET were the final source, you'd say, 'We're 40th, so that makes us a 10 seed.' That's not how it works. There's a tremendous amount of nuance to it. I think Bracketology is something you need to pay attention to, but if you pay so much attention to it that you lose your focus, that's not going to be a positive."

—Chris Mooney, Richmond head coach

"I pay attention to it as a fan with the understanding that it's not over until it's over. Because of that reality, I don't use it with our team at all. I'm happy to admit that I follow Bracketology as a fan. It's fun to watch and has become an important way for fans to connect with our game. But it has no bearing on our coaching."

—Jay Wright, Villanova head coach

"Probably. At the end of the day, they know it doesn't matter until the committee makes its selection. But they're going to use every bit of information they have to their advantage. If in the middle of January there's a mock bracket that has seven conference teams in it, including yours, why wouldn't you promote that? I don't think you should overreact if that bracket says you only have three teams in because it's only January. But if you're a school that appears to be part of the field, it certainly can't hurt your fan engagement, how you're positioning your program in recruiting, and the feeling around the program."

—Vince Nicastro, Big East deputy commissioner/COO

"I paid attention even when I wasn't on the committee because I love the game of basketball and I knew Joe. It was interesting. It's great because it promotes the game of basketball. It's well done by ESPN because of Joe. He has a personality that you want to believe. You know he's done his homework. I believe coaches pay attention. They're part of the general public. Coaches are fans, too."

—Tom O'Connor, former George Mason athletic director, 2008 Selection Committee chair

"There's no doubt in my mind that coaches pay attention. We all talk about it—who's projected in, who's out, who's on the bubble, what the projected seeds are, etc."

—Steve Watson, Loyola Chicago athletic director

"Through the years Joe has proven that he's very accurate at picking the teams and even the seeds. As I got into coaching, it's something that I really paid attention to. When we'd have a big win, we'd look to see if we moved up any seed lines. I remember one of our really good years [2004–05], we only lost two games in the entire season. Joe had us as a top four seed. We were going, 'This is awesome.' We lost the championship game in the Big West Tournament, and the Big West has historically been a one-bid league. Joe had us solidly in, so we knew we were going to make it, no matter what happened. When we lost, we dropped a bunch of seed lines. I remember wondering if we had scheduled enough or over-scheduled. We ended up getting in but as an 8 seed. We beat Pittsburgh but then lost to No. 1 seed Washington."

—Aaron Woliczko, West Coast Conference administrator
and former University of the Pacific assistant coach

From a conference perspective, how does Bracketology help you?

"Especially for leagues like ours, which are multiple-bid leagues, it creates more transparency about the process. That informs the schools how to schedule and position themselves for selection. I don't know that it's a direct result of Bracketology, but I think there's been a much greater focus on how the selection process works, and schools are being responsive to that. It's more intentional. At the end of the day, tournament participation is one of our primary strategic objectives to maximize the number of teams we get into the NCAA Tournament and to get them to build their seed lines. The better their seed, the higher the probability they're going to advance.

"We use the selection and seeding criteria and protocols that the NCAA has developed to help inform the choices our schools make. You can call that Bracketology. I don't know that they use what Joe does, but they certainly use the same principles he uses. As a conference we've developed scheduling alliances with other conferences to assure that our schools are scheduling non-conference games that maximize opportunities for the NCAA Tournament. We have relationships with the Big Ten and the Big 12."

—*Vince Nicastro, Big East deputy commissioner/COO*

"We're all vying for spots in the NCAA Tournament, and that's the starting point. Early in the season, we're looking at his posts weekly. As the season goes on, we look daily. If he says in his too early field that the WCC is going to have three teams, I'm expected to promote that fact. My role is the day-to-day operations of men's basketball for the conference. One of the biggest aspects is to increase national exposure. Basically, Bracketology helps. When I look at Bracketology and see that Joe has us with multiple teams in the NCAA Tournament, we know that it's going to be a good year. Our conference is a non-football conference. We make our money from the revenue that's generated from the teams in the tournament…Every time a team from our conference gets into the tournament, that provides revenue we can distribute to our members."

—*Aaron Woliczko, West Coast Conference administrator and former University of the Pacific assistant coach*

What do you think of Joe Lunardi's accuracy as a bracketologist?

"It's amazing how accurate he is. It's truly amazing how close he gets it. Who gets in—that's pretty easy. But where they're seeded, that's remarkable how accurate he is, especially when they changed the criteria."

—*Bob Huggins, West Virginia head coach*

"Oh, sure, I think what he does best is base his opinions on the history of the committee. He values what they value. I think he values conference records. If you have a record under .500 in the conference, you shouldn't get in. Being a guy who grew up in the world of the mid-major with the Atlantic 10, he puts more value on a great mid-major team than a better-than-average high-major team. But he knows that the committee doesn't see it that way and he makes very educated picks based on that, which is very good for college basketball."

—*Chris Mooney, Richmond head coach*

"Joe is a basketball junkie and he really works at it. When you really work at something and delve into it, you can come up with some pretty good statistics. He looks at it more than most people, and then he presents it in a way that's readable. There are other people out there who do the same thing, but Joe does his job well. It's a labor of love."

—*Tom O'Connor, former George Mason athletic director, 2008 Selection Committee chair*

"Who Joe has in the tournament is not as important to me as their seed level. I looked at who he had in and who I thought should be in—to look for outliers. If Joe had someone different than I did, I tried to figure out why. Sometimes I'd pick up the phone and ask him. In all my years on the committee, we only had discussions about a handful of teams [from] the Last Four In and the First Four Out. We probably looked at 10 or 12. Some were obviously not going to get in but were worth the discussion. I don't think being in or not being in is as important as the seeding. You can't improve your seed if you're not one of the 68. But it's critical to get them in the correct order. It is more of a full-time job for Joe than it is for a lot of committee members. It's difficult for a committee member to know the strengths of a member of a one-bid conference and to know how they compare to the others in the same bucket—the 14, 15, and 16 seeds. To have someone like Joe spend a lot of time at it, who not only uses data and observation—and you need a good balance—is important. I think Joe's value is much greater in the seeding part of it than the selection part of it."

—Bruce Rasmussen, Creighton athletic director, 2018 Selection Committee chair

"He is very accurate because he works very hard. That's why I have so much respect for him."

—Dick Vitale, ESPN college basketball analyst

Is Joe Lunardi good for college basketball?

"Absolutely, no question. He's good for the tournament. Everybody is watching it. Not just coaches but fans. I get so many texts from our boosters and fans. It's not something you can block out. It's part of the NCAA culture. There are other people doing it, [but] no one is more well-known than Joe. And because it causes people to talk about the tournament, it's good for college basketball. It draws people in who may not be drawn in otherwise. People want to know what's going to happen before it happens, and he's giving them a high-percentage prediction."

—*Randy Bennett, St. Mary's head coach*

"Yes, first of all, he's passionate about the game. He loves the game and he helps promote the game and the teams. College basketball is all about the teams. It is a way for people to get excited about and build up to March Madness. He's been good for the tournament and college basketball in that way."

—*Dan Gavitt, NCAA men's basketball senior vice president and son of Big East founder Dave Gavitt*

"First of all, Joe Lunardi is an entertainer. He understands the entertainment aspect of what he does. He's got the personality for it. He's like a cartoon character. He embraces that.

Secondly, he creates conversation. That's good for the game. I was at the University of Miami when they brought back basketball and later when the Miami Heat became a reality. I remember thinking that it would cause people to talk about basketball, and the more people talk about basketball, the better it is. Joe creates the conversation, the debate, the dialogue. Any time you move the needle, that's a good thing. To me his greatness is that he takes himself—and his job— seriously, but he can laugh about himself as well. Those are two really good traits."

—Seth Greenberg, ESPN analyst
and former Virginia Tech head coach

"One thousand percent. The most glamorous and exciting part of college basketball is the NCAA Tournament, and he keeps the NCAA Tournament in the front of everyone's mind throughout the whole season. You're always talking about whether this team is in or out or whether that team is a No. 1 seed or a No. 2 seed. I think that is really great promotion for college basketball."

—Chris Mooney, Richmond head coach

"He is for sure. He was the first one to lift the veil and urge the transparency of selection and seeding. I think that was good. The fan engagement piece is year-round. Those of us who are practitioners understand that the mock brackets in

April, May, and June don't matter much. They don't impact the committee at all. But they get the fans of those schools talking about their teams and their possible matchups."

—*Vince Nicastro, Big East deputy commissioner/COO*

"Absolutely! Joe has built a great reputation not just during the season but all during the year. His comments are great motivating signals. My predictions are not so scientific, but I do try to predict according to what I have seen on the various courts."

—*Sister Jean Dolores-Schmidt, Loyola Chicago chaplain*

"Absolutely. Who would say he's not good? What negative is he doing? You might disagree with him and you have a right to do that. I respect it when people disagree with me. We don't have a license to tell people they can't disagree. But what damage can he do? You might check Joe's brackets and others' as well. Then you form your own opinion. He gives me a good guiding light, but I'm still going to form my own opinion. My way of judging—the VBDI [Vitale Bald Dome Index]—helps me to form my opinion. The eye test works well. I enjoy having conversations with Joe during telecasts regarding certain teams. He's very up front and honest in the way he does his evaluations. You might not agree with him, but he's going to tell you what he believes and what he can document."

—*Dick Vitale, ESPN college basketball analyst*

"He's the pioneer, the original bracketologist. Because of his knowledge and his track record, he's built up credibility in the basketball world and gives us all a look inside the selection process."

—*Steve Watson, Loyola Chicago athletic director*

"I think Joe is one of the best people for college basketball. His heart is in the right place. It absolutely destroys me—because I think of Joe as a friend—when he says something against a team, and he gets blasted. He's just being honest. His research of saying that Team X is no longer a No. 1 seed is based on fact. The fanbase will go crazy. It hurts me to see that. But Joe takes it so well. He knows it's part of the job. People think Joe has something to do with the actual selections because he's that good."

—*Aaron Woliczko, West Coast Conference administrator and former University of the Pacific assistant coach*

"Joe Lunardi is great for college basketball. His work spikes interest in our game throughout the year."

—*Jay Wright, Villanova head coach*

Now in case this sounds like we're getting a little too rosy about my work and Bracketology, I present to you what Indiana coach Archie Miller said. The Hoosiers had just lost their home finale to Wisconsin to close the Big

Ten season, dropping to 19–12 overall and 9–11 in conference play. Interestingly, even after that loss, I still had the Hoosiers as a Last Four In. Apparently, that wasn't enough.

Here's Miller's extended response after that loss: "If you watch *Sesame Street* and listen to all of the characters on *Sesame Street* talk, everyone gets all [worked up]. It's like if you watch *Sesame Street*, you listen to the guys on *Sesame Street*. It's a children's show. Every bracketologist is a children's show. Bottom line: we know [what] our resume is—strength of record—and that's undeniable. It's a Top 25 strength of record. You don't not put in a Top 25 strength of record team with the wins that we have—somebody's going to have to answer some questions. Maybe we didn't win on the road. All right, there's about 15 teams that didn't do that. Well, there's some teams that have maybe half the amount of Quad One wins that we have. And when you look at our wins, I think we have three wins against the top 10 in the quad. Two-seed Florida State, we beat this team. Since December 3rd we have not played one team that's not a high-major team. No one's done it. But when you start to go through the Bracketology and listen to the *Sesame Street* cartoon guys on TV, you need people to click and all this stuff, the bottom line is strength of record. Who'd you play? Who'd you beat? And if you look at our wins, there's very few teams in the country that can say they've beaten Florida

State, Michigan State, Ohio State, Iowa, Penn State, who are clearly in the field. So if you're beating six, seven teams in the field, you should be in the field.

"Now, everyone's going to say, 'You don't have a .500 record in the league.' They've already stated that a .500 record in the league doesn't matter. It's your body of work because there's certain teams that played the 330th non-conference strength of schedule, which we didn't do. If you add it all up, we scheduled to make the tournament. We've got a lot of good wins, played in an unprecedented season in the Big Ten in terms of depth. And when you add that many teams competing for the tournament—12—most of the year and you beat each other up, my hope is that they just don't take it for granted: how hard it is to win in the league. And I think today was our 24th or 25th straight Power Five game. I mean, who does that? We did."

It's all good, Coach, but I can't imagine what you would have said if your team was First Four Out.

CHAPTER TEN

My Crystal Ball

The future of Bracketology is inextricably linked to the future of college basketball. And the future of college basketball—the future of all college sports, for that matter—is ultimately linked to the future of college football. In the modern era of intercollegiate athletics, almost every major shift in the landscape has been a byproduct of decisions made regarding college football. Conference realignment confirms that fact. You can't tell me West Virginia basketball is better served with a home-and-home against Texas Tech than it would be with a home-and-home against Pitt. Similar examples prevail in every region of the country.

Conferences realigned to cash in on television opportunities. It was all about maximizing eyeballs and their respective geographic footprints. Most of the traditional multi-bid basketball leagues now have TV networks of their own. These networks operate with varying degrees of success, depending on market size and the success of teams on the field and court. The Big Ten Network works. The SEC Network works. The ACC Network works. Most of that modeling took place with football in mind.

The dollars involved in major college football dwarf those of basketball or any other sport. Why else would Boston College send its women's soccer team to Clemson? When realignment was at its craziest, there was a brief period—though it never resulted in a season on the field—when Boise State and San Diego State were members of the Big East's football conference. I remember joking to myself, *I guess Hawaii wasn't available.*

In basketball there have been periodic flirtations between the Big East and Gonzaga. You can't get much less "East" than Spokane, Washington, but the Zags certainly qualify as "Big." As a conference of primarily private, Catholic, basketball-only schools, the Big East model would be a great fit for Gonzaga in that aspect. But the next-closest school for Gonzaga would be Creighton (in Omaha, Nebraska,) a mere 1,433 miles away. The logistics just don't work, especially for non-revenue sports. Even basketball would be a stretch. How do the Zags play at Villanova on a Wednesday night and have any kind of normal college life for their student-athletes? College football teams only travel every other week. The arguments are similar to those made about having an NFL team in London. How far is too far? Some West Coast NFL teams stay east when they have back-to-back East Coast road games or vice versa, and their players don't have to worry about getting up for class. The rigors and occasional unpredictability of travel are real, especially for winter sports. And there are obvious differences between 30-year-old professionals and 18-year-old student-athletes.

In college football the first big domino to fall was when Penn State joined the Big Ten in 1990. Things really started to roll when Nebraska went to the Big Ten in 2011, and I remember snickering to myself when the Nebraska chancellor said something like, "We look forward to our faculty and graduate schools joining the Big Ten research consortium." What he no doubt meant to say was the Cornhuskers were looking for bigger payouts from the Big Ten and Big Ten Network, not to mention the Rose Bowl. So don't insult our intelligence by sugarcoating blatant—and in many cases sensible—financial decisions.

Football wealth also creates layers of inequality throughout the college sports landscape. It's hard to fault Penn State giving up its independent status for the Big Ten gold mine or Notre Dame remaining independent to preserve a lucrative NBC contract. None of the money in major college football flows through the NCAA. Television contracts are negotiated mainly at the conference level. The only role for the NCAA is compliance, and there is nothing sexy (or lucrative) about that. So it's no surprise that Kansas and Missouri saw their basketball rivalry disappear. Nobody got in a room and said, "It's good for basketball for those teams not to play anymore." We all know football was the driving force behind Missouri's move to the SEC.

The only clear example in the modern era of a school putting basketball ahead of football is the University of Connecticut. UConn's decision to return to the Big East seemed inevitable. The Huskies desperately wanted the ACC or another power conference to take their football team, but it never happened. The powers-that-be at UConn came to realize that bus trips to Providence were better than waiting and hoping to get in a football league with Florida State or Kansas State. Perhaps one of the 15 national championship banners—four in men's basketball, 11 more in women's basketball—finally fell on their collective heads.

Someday, maybe after the next pandemic, there will be football-only alliances with conferences playing regionally in every other sport. For now that doesn't work for the Big Ten or SEC Network. They need year-round programming. Football pays the bills, but softball helps fill all the other hours.

Because of football the haves are separating further from the have-nots. This has a direct impact on Bracketology. It is now permissible to compensate student-athletes over and above tuition, room and board, books, etc. They receive what amounts to walking-around money. But if Michigan or Ohio State determine cost of attendance and pay it out at significantly higher rates than Central Michigan or Ohio University, the competitive distance between Michigan and Central Michigan or Ohio State and Ohio is going to increase exponentially.

One assumes that if the football factories had their way, the NCAA's men's basketball championship would include only teams from the power conferences. The only thing the Big Ten would like more than giving one bid to the Mid-American Conference would be giving them zero bids. There are years in which 32 or 33 of the 36 at-large spots go to five or six leagues. At almost $2 million a pop, why not control everything? You can certainly understand the rationale. *We're the ones making the largest investment in this enterprise, whether it's scholarships, facilities, coaches' salaries, corporate money, television deals, etc. Why shouldn't we reap the greatest return on our investment?*

When UMBC beat Virginia in 2018, becoming the first No. 16 seed to defeat a No. 1 seed in the NCAA Tournament, the on-court gap was considerable. The off-court gap was far greater. The only time UVA gets on a bus is for a short ride to a charter flight. UMBC never gets off the bus. The Cavaliers aren't doing anything wrong. They're just playing a different game. What's holding it all together is what I like to call the "Cinderella factor." Paying the enormous rights fees for the Division I men's basketball championship, the networks seem to know the public is more interested in watching George Mason make a Final Four run than the 10th best team in the SEC. At least in the early rounds of the tournament, more of us watch Sister Jean than Oregon State. Cinderella can and often does win in college basketball. CBS and Turner are prime beneficiaries.

That's not so in football, or at least rarely so. The worst team in the Big Ten would stomp the best team in the Patriot League every time. The athletes are bigger, stronger, faster. They're grain-fed behemoths who in normal times are on campus every month of the year. There are no grain silos at Lehigh. Why watch if you already know the outcome? Eventually, the same thing will happen in college basketball. The financial gap will bring an end to Cinderella, and her clock will strike midnight permanently. As the gap widens, the current structure of Division I men's basketball may become untenable, if it's not already.

In the '50s and '60s, basketball was an afterthought, and football was the lone money-maker for most of the big state schools. Now that hoops generate a fair share of revenue, everyone wants to be in the game. Will the sport—and by extension Bracketology—be damaged as the Cinderella factor disappears? Who will be the upstarts? The underdogs? Who is the No. 12 seed that can beat a No. 5? What double-digit seeds will make the Sweet 16? When Steph Curry was at Davidson and his Wildcats played Kansas in the 2008 Elite Eight, it was a huge draw. Does that game have the same magnitude if Curry is at Clemson? He would have just been another great ACC player there. As crazy as it seems, he would not have been considered the best player in his own conference. Tyler Hansbrough of North Carolina won ACC Player of the Year in 2008 and deservedly so. The point isn't to debate a hypothetical award but to note that Curry at Davidson drew more people to the NCAA Tournament than a Curry at Clemson or South Carolina would have.

The 2020 NCAA Tournament will go down as the greatest tourney never played. But we can feel pretty certain that Obi Toppin of Dayton and Malachi Flynn of San Diego State would have drawn in more casual fans—just like even non-Kansas folks remember Northern Iowa's shooting guard from 2010. *Give it up for Ali Farokhmanesh!* If a player is at Zion Williamson's level, that's a different story. Everyone tunes in. But there are 10 really good players a year who never move the needle. When a Toppin comes along even once a decade, it adds untold value. The freshness of the non-perennial schools and their stars is a gigantic part of college basketball's charm. If and when the sport breaks apart—like the old I-A and I-AA divisions in college football—it may bring in more revenue for fewer participants. But it will be a bad and sad day for the sport in the long run.

You can't tell me that a Thursday afternoon first-round game between Texas A&M and Oregon State would be more captivating than Lehigh's 2012 upset of Duke. That's what could be lost if we're not careful stewards of the game. Bracketology would still exist, and we'd apply the same rigor and analytics to seeding the last-place team in the Pac-12. It just wouldn't be as much fun.

I don't think the big breakup happens in my professional lifetime, but I think there is at least a 50/50 chance we see it in my physical lifetime. And it makes me sad. The power conferences will still need non-league opponents. So the American Athletic Conference, Atlantic 10, and Mountain West are probably okay. But there are no guarantees if the asteroid ever hits. The big boys will set the rules. The power conferences will negotiate their own TV contracts, including the postseason—just like the Power Five and Notre Dame negotiate football contracts. That's the model. If there are 64 spots in a championship tournament and each spot is worth $2 million, those entities, those conferences, those schools in the top tier won't want to give half of it away. The only Blue Devils will be from Duke, not Central Connecticut.

The big football schools are sharks and they may even be right. Division I is probably too large by about a hundred or so schools. The former are taking every opportunity to make college basketball too expensive for the latter. The big boys keep pushing more of their chips to the center of the table, forcing the next-tier schools to match. Whether it is cost of attendance, charter flights, training rooms and nutrition, extra staff, or whatever the case may be, they're going to price the Mom and Pop operations out of the market. There won't be an NCAA Tournament with Florida Gulf Coast and Vermont, at least as we've come to know it.

Bracketology would be dramatically impacted as well. People won't likely care as much about Mississippi State's projected seed when the Bulldogs finish 12th in the SEC but still get in the tournament. I'm fearful of that, and it's why I frequently advocate for measures that would keep the playing field a little more even. Call it affirmative action, if you will, but for minority schools. I believe in the long run that the argument for the mid-majors will be lost, and the sport will be at a loss because of it. College basketball and the NCAA Tournament are filled with too many great tales from Bill Russell at San Francisco and Larry Bird at Indiana State all the way through Gordon Hayward at Butler and Toppin at Dayton.

In the meantime, as long as there are non-football schools in Division I basketball, they should have some legislative protection. Just as teams need to become bowl eligible in college football, there needs to be a tournament eligibility standard. I'd humbly offer the "Lunardi Rule," requiring a

.500 record in conference play to be eligible for an at-large bid. From a fan and interest perspective, I would let teams count conference tournament games. If you're 8–10 in the regular season and win twice in your league tourney, the Lunardi Rule doesn't apply. You've made yourself tournament eligible by getting back to .500.

The committee doesn't even look at conference record as part of its current process. Conference records do not appear on the team sheets. This makes no sense unless the reason is to exclude a valid data point that might adversely affect a handful of overrated power schools. If we trust the committee to understand non-conference scheduling, disproportionate home/road splits, players absences, and the like, surely they can discern whether or not Oklahoma and its 7–11 conference record should be under consideration.

The counterargument is that teams shouldn't be punished for losing too many games in a great league, which never has and never will make sense to me. We keep score for a reason. This isn't everybody gets a trophy. The scale has tipped too far. When regular-season champions of the top dozen or so conferences are being left out of the championship field despite proving over 30-plus games that they're good enough to win home and away, I can't justify taking a team that goes 2–9 over the last month. There are other practices that artificially tip the scale. The expansion of mega-conferences and the oversized league schedules they are adopting deprive teams outside those conferences of the opportunity to actually play. It's bad enough that non-majors almost always have to play these games on the road or at best in a neutral event, but now the games are disappearing entirely. A more closed system has been created for the elite.

The big boys aren't dumb. They also know an increase in conference games will boost the resumes of their mediocre teams. Even a bad team in a good league is going to win a few Quad One games if it gets that many chances, especially at home. Remember: the *average* Division I team wins 70 percent of its home games. Middling majors can't help but pile up opportunities and wins disproportionately under these circumstances. The New York Yankees can't have a bad loss if they only play the Boston Red Sox and never the Baltimore Orioles.

We have the data. Sub-.500 major conference teams get more bids and better seeds than their mid-major, at-large counterparts. But they lose in the tournament almost three times as often in spite of their bracketing advantages. Logic suggests we might want to look at that type of team in a broader sense. If over a 10-year period, two-thirds of the No. 1 seeds didn't reach the second weekend, we might say it's time to reevaluate the criteria of the top seeds. Something would have gone wrong. If a similar examination of bubble-team data and performance resulted in something equally out of whack—which it has—we should look at that, too. If the Lunardi Rule was adopted, would there be deserving major conference teams who occasionally didn't make it? Yes. But there wouldn't be nearly as many of them as the current omissions among the top mid-majors. It's all in the data.

Three years ago Loyola Chicago was losing at halftime of its Missouri Valley Conference quarterfinal. The Ramblers were 25–5 going into that game. Given the No. 11 seed they received *after winning the MVC tournament*, they may not have made the NCAAs had they lost that MVC Tournament game. What a colossally bad system, and I'm willing to die on that hill for saying so. For a very good team in a good mid-major league to win 30 times, it has to win *a lot* of road games. It's much harder to do that as a matter of probability than it is to win two or three Quad One home games in a power conference. I'm going to keep pointing this out until someone shuts me up or until the mid-majors stop winning NCAA Tournament games. The scale needs to be re-balanced.

The public also understands winning. A large sample online poll preferred the Lunardi Rule by a 60/40 margin over sub-.500 conference teams making the tournament. Also, we're only talking about one or two bids per year. Is the world going to stop spinning on its axis if St. Bonaventure makes the NCAAs over a Big Ten team that went 7–13 in the league? It boils down to the simplest question possible: if fill-in-the-blank middling major is really good enough, why didn't it win another game or two? Until somebody can answer that in a satisfactory manner, I would rather err on the side of 29–4 St. Mary's.

* * *

What's right about college basketball and what's not? What's most right on an individual level is that college basketball is a true meritocracy. You can either play or you can't. It doesn't matter if you're rich or poor; Black or white; Catholic, Jewish, or Protestant; Republican or Democrat; or you come from the East Coast, West Coast, or somewhere in between. This is certainly true in every sport, but formative images of basketball are powerful. Jimmy Chitwood shooting jumpers on a dirt farm in Indiana is just as meaningful as the kid playing on the asphalt courts of Harlem. A basketball, a hoop, and a pair of shoes are all that's necessary for everyone to play the same game. Basketball at almost every level has become a microcosm of society nationally and internationally. Spend enough time around a well-organized basketball team, and it's hard not to be affirmed about society at large.

We cannot and should not undervalue shared purpose and teamwork as common attributes of success. They're all valuable and should be lauded at every opportunity.

Ultimately, basketball is a pretty simple game. One ball, five guys, and let's go. Good coaching is certainly an asset, but most, if not all, would agree that if the Golden State Warriors, when they were led by Steph Curry and Kevin Durant, had to give up their coaching staff, trainer, weight room, and charter plane, they'd still wipe the floor with the New York Knicks. The game has a flow that supersedes amenities. The best coaches are the ones who enhance the flow and get out of the way.

Basketball is also a game of underappreciated skills, not one dominated by brute force strength or God-given speed. Shooting is a finesse skill. Great shooters can be tall or short, skinny or fat, fast or slow. You can either get to the rim off the dribble or you can't. Obviously, bigger guys typically block more shots and get more rebounds, but the little guy—figuratively or literally—can more than hold his or her own. The game even allows for a certain individualism almost like a batting stance. We mimic how certain guys release their jumper, spin off free throws, or other mannerisms. I have friends who imitate how certain referees make a key call. There is some of that in the NFL but not nearly as much.

All of which is not to diminish the physical nature of the game. LeBron James is a freight train with incredible strength, mobility, and dexterity. He may be one of the greatest pure athletes of all time. It's incredibly compelling to see that kind of size and strength channeled into the finesse required for the best parts of basketball. James, for instance, is a fabulous passer. In crunch time of Game 7, he's as likely to pass as go to the basket. You knew when Michael Jordan was on the court, he was taking the last shot. Not always with James. Kobe Bryant? Yes. Larry Bird? Maybe not.

Players who are willing to share the ball are popular at every level, including the pick-up game. We've all played with ball hogs. I'm always struck by the term "volume shooter." Isn't that just a nicer way of saying ball hog? Allen Iverson was the 2001 NBA MVP, the first pick in the 1996 NBA Draft, and a perennial All-Star. But other than one season, in which the Philadelphia 76ers reached the NBA Finals, he was a round peg in a square hole, a nearly impossible star around which to build a champion. The Sixers tried every conceivable cast of characters and coaches with A.I., and nothing worked for very long. There is only one ball on the court, and for Iverson to shine, he had to have it. The best basketball ever played is the opposite of that, whether it was John Wooden's UCLA teams, Golden State's Splash

Brothers, or the unending Boston Celtics dynasty. Nine times out of 10, five is better than one.

That's easier said than done, of course. Basketball's ongoing struggle between individual and group is metaphorical more than most other sports. In football if my guys can knock down your guys, I'm going to gain more yardage. It's not very subtle. Basketball is our version of soccer. One ball and individual athletic expression are the hallmark of both sports. It doesn't matter who shows up or where you are. Whether it's Madison Square Garden, Allen Fieldhouse, or the driveway, if you have a ball and a few players, it's game on. It's the same in soccer. You need a patch of ground and a ball. By nature baseball and certainly football need more people and equipment.

Another great thing about college basketball in particular is its enthusiasm. Dick Vitale's passion shows up when he calls the game. Can you imagine an announcer crowd-surfing at an NBA or NFL game? Unlike professional sports, which are limited mostly to major cities by economic necessity, just about everyone has a college team or teams they root for. It's where they went to school or where their dad, sister, or crazy Uncle Steve went. They've been hearing about good ol' State U since they were kids.

Is there too much money in the game? Is it too commercial? Should Zion Williamson even be in college? All are legitimate questions. Reasonable people can disagree about the answers. In Division I college basketball, there are 357 schools multiplied by 13 scholarships per team, giving us close to 5,000 student-athletes in the sport each year. Each has a story. For the vast majority of them, the NBA or any high-level professional basketball isn't a realistic option. After the last loss of their senior year, the only game in town might be Sunday night at the rec center. The fleeting nature of the college game combined with the fact that there are rooting interests in all 50 states, as opposed to just the major pro markets, makes the fan experience more personal.

For the other students on campus, the players on the court not only represent their school, but they also might be in their Econ 101 class. Even if said star is asleep in that class, you're surely going to brag about your classmate at Thanksgiving dinner. It can be the same in any sport, but football players wear helmets and don't get many close-ups. We don't really even see them unless they're among the few who get a lot of TV time. In basketball it's just as often a late-game substitute on the foul line with a second to go as it is the star. We remember the aforementioned Ali Farokhmanesh but not because he was a 10-time NBA All-Star. We can't even spell his name without looking it up. He had a moment. Every year we never know which of the 5,000 stories are going to end up as part of "One Shining Moment."

But there are some danger zones in the sport we love. There is clearly a competitive imbalance. It may be inevitable and it could one day result in future haves and have-nots divisions. For the moment there is only one Division I. I don't think it's good for the game when certain schools are able to buy themselves a head start. What do I mean by that? At one extreme of Division I, there are schools starting the season 10–0 because they are All-American check-writers. Too many schools start 0–10 because they can only survive by cashing those checks. We now have pretty good ways to measure 10–0 versus 0–10, but the casual observer only sees where the zero is. I can't think of another sport with such an overt imbalance. There is a caste system before the ball goes up. It's a black eye for the game and speaks to other money problems in the sport.

College basketball players have been getting paid under the table for as long as there have been tables. Talent in any endeavor is going to be rewarded at some level commensurate with interest in that endeavor. If I could do card tricks better than anyone else in the world and walked around a casino with a sign proving that, people would probably throw poker chips at me to show them some card tricks. That's just the way it is. The purity and alleged amateurism of college sports are laudable but not realistic. If we want a sport, in which television pays billions of dollars to air the best games, there is going to be a secret economy. If we went back to the peach basket and playing only for the joy of the game, it might be wonderful, but there would be far fewer eyeballs. Just like the Olympics, once millions were interested in the 100 meters, the participants wanted a piece of the action.

What is a tolerable level of commercialism that doesn't sully the entire enterprise? Is it okay if Williamson's family got $100,000 to watch him blow out a sneaker at Duke? Today you can stay and play for as little as one year of college basketball. In college baseball once you go to your first class, you've got to stay three years. Maybe the issue isn't compensation. Should those players, who are truly worth six or seven figures, be in college at all? John McEnroe and Tiger Woods left Stanford early, and no one was worse for it—least of all them! Maybe it was actually more pure when top recruits could go straight to the NBA. We're going to end up back there in some way very soon.

As much as we may have wanted to see James or Bryant in college, the game was fine without them. The game was fine when Lew Alcindor couldn't play freshman ball. Heck, it added to Alcindor's legend when his freshman UCLA team beat the varsity, who were two-time defending national champions. Certain eligibility restrictions may be archaic. It wouldn't be the first time that happened.

Looking back, outlawing the dunk was silly, and allowing only half the team in girls' basketball to cross center court was draconian. People thought girls should only dribble so many times to prevent them from falling down or getting hurt. Have fun with that one today. We've all seen highlights of the old skinny foul lane or courts with no three-point line. They're from another time. We didn't used to have the forward pass in football. Goal posts blocked the end zone. I'm all for modernizing our games (including the universal designated hitter). There may never be a perfect middle ground in any endeavor, but that doesn't mean we stop looking for it. College basketball is no different. Where is the middle ground?

I'm not worried about losing more players to the professional ranks. Even if the top 10 recruits every year went to the NBA Developmental League, the ACC would easily outdraw the G League. The Delaware Blue Coats are better than the Duke Blue Devils, but I don't see the Blue Coats on TV every Wednesday and Saturday. They just don't have the brand. The game will overcome all of our efforts to screw it up.

The game is also good enough to overcome its inherent conflicts, but the NCAA's approach of ignoring problems and hoping they go away isn't helpful. I'll stay in my lane and speak only about the current postseason structure. We need to be proactive in addressing the manipulation of the NCAA Tournament by the power conferences before they take over the entire field.

It's time to consider a modest—*very* modest—expansion of the tournament. When the 64-team field came into being in 1985, Division I comprised 282 schools. Between the NCAA Tournament (64 teams) and the NIT (32 teams), the 96-team postseason included just over one-third of the Division I membership. For better or worse, we've added 75 Division I schools since then—but only four NCAA bids—dropping meaningful postseason participation to 28 percent of all teams. I'm not suggesting anything like major college football, where half of all Football Bowl Subdivision (FBS) teams go to bowl games, just an overdue tweak of the math.

My suggestion would be a 72-team NCAA Tournament. Two additional doubleheaders could easily be played on the Tuesday and Wednesday nights of the existing First Four. If modernizing while retaining competitive balance is the agreed-upon objective, an equal number of major and mid-major teams would be added. Form subgroups of the Selection Committee to pick the additional teams by category and play them off against one another. By Thursday noon a 64-team field would remain, and all would be right with the world. In my modeling there is a legitimate case for at least four additional teams, especially if more regular-season champions are included. But that's the cap. The we-almost-went-to-96-teams negotiations of 2010 proved as much.

One year on Selection Sunday, I came off the set after being on the air with Chris Fowler, Jay Bilas, and Digger Phelps. We had concluded the seemingly annual bubble debate over a high-major team and a mid-major. That year the debate was between Notre Dame and Siena. Digger barked as only he can, "If Notre Dame played in Siena's league, they would never lose."

I countered, "They would absolutely lose" because the Irish would have to play nine true road games, which happened to be nine more than they had played at any point of their non-conference season.

When I got back to the Green Room, who else but Bob Knight was waiting to go on for the next segment. I knew Coach Knight only in passing. So it was more than a little intimidating when he moved toward me with apparent purpose. He got right in my face and said, "Lunardi, why do you take that bullshit from those guys? Aren't you the one who's right all the time?" I answered, "Coach, that's very kind of you, but we really don't know who's better—Notre Dame or Siena—because they never play. And even if they did, it would never be on a neutral court."

Knight said, "I'm going to go in there and tell them that if we doubled the field to 128 teams, we'd stop all these stupid arguments. Would I be a jackass if I said that?" It was a little bit like when a woman asks her husband, "Does this dress make me look fat?" Somehow I didn't say what I was thinking.

I said, "Coach, I appreciate you asking, but let's remember that between us we have 902 coaching wins. And you have all of them." I, though, couldn't help but add: "It's a colossally bad idea. If I showed you team No. 127 or No. 128 right now, you'd throw a fit and say they have no business playing for a national championship."

"Thanks for setting me straight," Knight replied. "I don't want to look like an idiot out there." That's a true story. Of course, what's also true is that if the field was ever expanded to anything close to 128 teams, there would be an argument over who was No. 129.

There can't be many people observing the cut line like I do on a daily basis. If you're open-minded enough to look at the next tier of conferences—the Missouri Valley, the West Coast Conference, the Mid-American, or Conference USA—there are more teams than you think who are good enough to win in the NCAA Tournament. Heck, I want to do this long enough to see an at-large team from the Ivy League in the field. I don't think the competitive value and the integrity of the big dance would be hurt by doubling the First Four and going to 72 teams, especially if games outside the main bracket were limited to at-large teams only. No automatic qualifiers regardless of seed should have to play in to get to the field of 64. If you can earn an automatic bid—the key word being earn—you should be in the main bracket. The extended First Four should be comprised strictly of at-large selections. The best part of my tweaking would be the Tuesday/Wednesday drama. Removing AQs from the opening round would send only bubble teams to Dayton, Ohio, and whatever second site is selected. (I vote for the Palestra, by the way, which remains the greatest venue in the history of the sport.) All 16 teams from our bubble—Last Four Byes, Last Four In, First Four Out, Next Four Out—would be on the court where they belong to play for the final eight at-large spots in the main bracket.

I would consider expanding the NIT as well to something in the neighborhood of 40 or even 48 teams. I would get rid of the tournaments with the initials nobody remembers. Even with that kind of expansion, we'd have about one-third of all Division I teams in the postseason. And most will have won 20 games or more, which seems reasonable.

The NIT should be folded into the current Selection Show and all bracket contests. Call me crazy, but having two chances to win something is better than one, especially when your NCAA picks usually are blown to bits by dinnertime Thursday. Coaches and players are branded with a negative label for making the NIT. That doesn't make any sense to me. I know we'll never go back to the day where a school turns down an NCAA bid for the NIT, but finishing in the top-third of the sport should be more than a consolation prize. It could be structured like the higher level, non-playoff bowl games in college football. When the No. 8 team plays No. 12 in Orlando on New Year's Day, people watch. It's a big deal to win. We can make the NIT like that. Make the NIT regional championships a bigger deal. Move the NIT Final Four to Friday and Sunday at a separate, smaller arena in the NCAA Final Four city. With all those college basketball fans in town, it would be a built-in sellout. And the rest of us would watch.

However Bracketology shakes out in the future, the overwhelming feeling in the present is one of gratitude. It's a strange thing to become recognized for something that didn't exist a generation ago. What about a generation from now? It's impossible to say. I hope someone else is holding court from the Bracket Bunker. Someone younger, smarter, and more tech-savvy should be splitting the hairs of the bubble teams. My wish for that person is that they appreciate the opportunity and enjoy it as much as I have. He or she should appreciate the fans, too, as we sit beside them every night of every season. You're stuck with me for now. There are more games to watch, more seed lines to complete, and more memories to make. If the pandemic taught us anything, it should be an even greater appreciation for the here and now. In the meantime, may all your brackets be winners!

Acknowledgments

For many years I've religiously read the acknowledgments in other books. Not because I thought I'd ever write one, but because they often offer a window into the life and mind of the author.

For my first (and only?) book, I really want to get this right. This isn't the Oscars. No one is going to turn on a light and tell me I'm out of time. I can thank as many people as necessary. So here goes, by category.

Family comes first. My wife, Dr. Pamela Miller Lunardi, has been the best thing in my life since our first date in 1981, an event predictably postponed by ongoing commitments to that year's NCAA Tournament. She married me anyway in 1985, followed by the arrival of Emily (1994) and Elizabeth (1997). I love all three of my girls and am not ashamed to say I am the fourth best writer in the house.

My late parents, Hank and Carmela Lunardi, valued education and pushed us to always do our best. They were sticklers for the proper use of language, and if they could see me now, they would both say, "I can't believe they're paying him to talk." I have two older brothers—Henry, who took me to my first college basketball game in 1967, and Rich, who we lost to cancer in 2013. Remember how cool it was to idolize your older siblings? Me, too.

Trish, who married Henry, gave us Mark, Kathi, and Tim. Elaine, who married Rich, gave us Chris, Teresa, Jeffrey, and John. All of the spouses and grandchildren give my Dad a family tree of 48 Lunardis (and counting). Another few years and we may have our own field of 64.

A few extended family members must also be included: Uncle Mark, who always said more with less; the cool Ciccantelli cousins, plus Frank Surico; Aunt Anna, still repping the "whisper sisters" at 100 years young; and cousin Gary, who goes with Aunt Anna. Ted Miller, Pam's father, picked up where my Dad left off and, among other things, got me addicted to golf. In the furry friend department, Murray, Tucker, and now Sam have always championed the underdog.

Some guys are lucky to have one best friend. I have a bundle: Jim Schnepp, Mike Pierce, Kevin McAveney, Paul Morro, Jim Walsh, Joe Tierney, and Dennis Markopoulous. That's not including the golf crowd—Manny, John P., Krotee, Rob D., Bob D., and Chris Lewis—or the SAP dads: Michael Berkowitz, Andy Gross, Jim Moylan, and a guy named Chad. At various times, many of them have encouraged me to write a book. Some will even be able to read it.

Those who made my so-called "real job" at Saint Joseph's University so meaningful for so long: Fr. Nick Rashford,

Dan Hilferty, Kathy Gaval, Maureen Cullen, Marty Farrell, Katie Shields, Greg Dell'Omo, Joe DiAngelo, John Lord, Fr. Tim Lannon, John Smithson, Sarah Quinn, Fr. Kevin Gillespie, and Mark Reed. Those at SJU who suffered more than most in my employ: Tom Durso, Molly Harty, Maureen O'Connell, Bill Avington, Kelly Welsh, Carolyn Steigleman, Pat Allen, Coleen DeFruscio, Jeff Martin, Brooke Elser, and Kathy Cooke. You and many others succeeded in spite of the boss.

St. Joe's basketball is another huge bucket without which there is no launching pad to the wider world of the sport: Dr. Jack Ramsay, Don DiJulia, Jim Lynam, Jim Boyle, John Griffin, Phil Martelli, Geoff Arnold, Dave Duda, Mark Bass, Sully, Claire, Andy Doc, Larry Doc, Marie Wozniak, Billy Lange, Jill Bodensteiner, Jim Brown, Eileen Brown, Renie Shields, and the third floor of Barry Hall. Every broadcast partner for more than 1,100 games, especially Ken Krsolovic, Dan Baker, Tom McCarthy, and Matt Martucci. Thanks for letting me talk (or—in Ken's case—interrupt).

I was a sportswriter once, and more than a few editors and colleagues have opened doors or shown me a thing or two: Bob Vetrone, Bob Wright, Boop, Dick Weiss, Jack Scheuer, Dick Jerardi, Mike Kern, Ray Parrillo, Chic Riebel, Bob Tennant, Tom McNichol, Greg Greenday, Terry Toohey, Jack McCaffery, Rich Hoffman, Mike Jensen, Joe Juliano, and Marc Narducci. If you can cover a high school football game in the pouring rain or make deadline after a 9:00 PM tip at McGonigle Hall, you can do anything in this business.

The *Blue Ribbon* years were instrumental, of course, with Chris Wallace, Chris Dortch, and Diane Swiger. Thanks to you I got to know and love Buckhannon, West Virginia, and Chattanooga, Tennessee. Thanks to the original "bunker boys"—Durso, Avington, Charlie Creme, Bill Doherty—and the unsung heroes of our tournament preview edition, Dom Roberti and Paul Chambers (who was a good player and a better printer). Their digital successors—Duffy Ross, Paul Morro, and Jeff Martin—helped bring the tournament guide to life for ESPN.com. RIP, Duffy.

Which brings us to ESPN, where I run the greatest risk of leaving someone out (but still have to try). In alphabetical order, past and present, thanks to: Mark Adams, Rob Adamski, David Albright, Adam Amin, Jeff Anderson, Debbie Antonelli, Claire Atkins, Matt Bartley, Kim Belton, Roxy Bernstein, Paul Biancardi, Jay Bilas, Jason Benetti, Jeff Borzello, Jim Bowdon, Adrian Branch, Tom Brennan, John Brickley, Ron Buck, Doris Burke, Abbey Carnivale, David Ceisler, Jonathan Coachman, Mike Corey, Mike Couzens, Tom Crean, Dan Dakich, Rece Davis, Tom DeCorte, Mike Diesenhof, David Duffey, Jeff Dufine, Tim Dwyer, Jimmy Dykes, Brett Edgerton, Josh Elliott, LaPhonso Ellis,

Acknowledgments

Len Elmore, Mike Epstein, Sean Farnham, Chris Farrow, Daymeon Fishback, Dave Flemming, Lee Fitting, Jason Fitz, Chris Fowler, Bart Fox, Fran Fraschilla, Drew Gallagher, Bo Garret, Dino Gaudio, Andy Glockner, Meg Green, Doug Gottlieb, Bill Graff, Seth Greenberg, Scott Gustafson, Stos Hall, Hembo, Major Howe, Malcolm Huckaby, Robbie Hummel, Andy Katz, Marc Kestecher, Mel Kiper, David Kraft, Joshua Kramer, Steve Lavin, Kara Lawson, Mike Leber, Rob Lemley, Rebecca Lobo, Nick Loucks, Pat Lowry, Rachel Marcus, Jason McCallum, Sean McDonough, Baron Miller, Myron Medcalf, Tony Moss, Shawn Murphy, Brent Musburger, Kevin Negandhi, Anna Negron, Conor Nevins, Dari Nowkhah, Steve Oling, Dave Pasch, Steve Peresman, Digger Phelps, Nick Pietruszkiewicz, Tom Penders, Mark Plansky, Mark Preisler, Chris Ramsay, Karl Ravech, Bernie Ritter, Chris Riviezzo, Craig Robinson, Jeff Ross, Barry Sacks, Boog Sciambi, Matt Schick, Howie Schwab, Rosa Scott, Doug Sherman, Mike Shiffman, Anish Shroff, Dan Shulman, Miles Simon, Chris Spatola, Stanford Steve, Sam Strong, Tim Sullivan, Jillian Thaw, Keith Thursby, Brian Tully, Scott Van Pelt, Dick Vitale, Jason Vonick, Carol Voronyak, Bill Walton, Pete Watters, Tim Welsh, Corey Williams, Jay Williams, Talaya Wilkins, Chuck Wilson, Jeff Wilson, Bob Wischusen, Mark Wise, Brian Wong, Leslie Wymer, and, Ryan Yocum.

More basketball folks: Randy Bennett, Ron Bertovich, Mike Bobinski, Ray Cella, Tom Carroll, Joe Castiglione, Ed Cooley, Jay DeFruscio, Jamie Dixon, Steve Donahue, Bryce Drew, Scott Drew, Drew Dickerson, Matt Doherty, Mike Doyle, Fran Dunphy, Doug Elgin, Mark Few, John Feinstein, Travis Ford, Marcus Fuller, Paul Hightower, Langston Galloway, Dan Gavitt, Ray Giacoletti, John Giannini, Tom Holmoe, Sydney Johnson, Sean Kearney, Tim Kenny, Tim Krueger, Steve Lappas, Mike Matoso, Bernadette McGlade, Chris Mooney, Jameer Nelson, Vince Nicastro, Tom O'Connor, Tom Odjakjian, Bruce Rasmussen, Ryan Reggiani, Mark Schmidt, Greg Shaheen, Neil Sullivan, Mike Slive, Ricky Stokes, David Walsh, Aaron Woliczko, David Worlock, Jay Wright, and the referee who T'd me up in my first game as a winless CYO coach.

Others without a category (some of whom don't even know how influential they were): Barbara Busse, Bobby Clarke, Fr. Peadar Cronin, Damien High School, Harry Dietzler, Chris DiJulia, Mike Hare, Bill James, Malvern Retreat House, Randy Miller, Joe Sheehan, Sr. Michael Mary, Joe "Pope" Sullivan, Fr. Pat Travers, Mark Whicker, Harry Young, and the Agonis Club of Dayton.

Last but certainly not least, coauthor David Smale, agent Maury Gostfrand, and the good folks at Triumph Books. I am delighted to be your teammate. Thank you.